KU-009-292

The Learning Curve
Allan Glen's Building
Central College of Commerce
190 Cathedral Street
Glasgow
G4 0ND
Tel 0141 271 6240

Contents

Contents

INSTITUTE OF LEADERSHIP & MANAGEMENT

SUPER**SERIES**

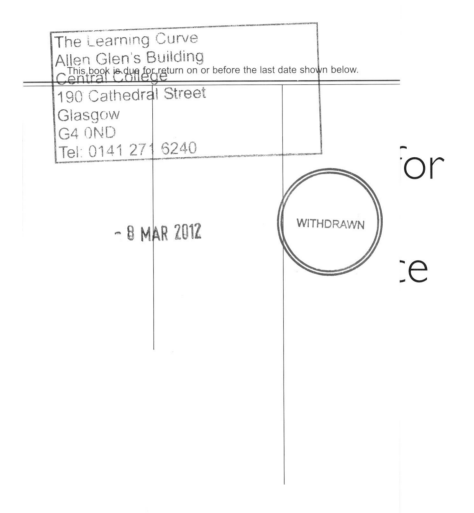

or

e

Published for the
Institute of Leadership & Management by

Pergamon
Flexible
Learning

OXFORD   AMSTERDAM   BOSTON   LONDON   NEW YORK   PARIS
SAN DIEGO   SAN FRANCISCO   SINGAPORE   SYDNEY   TOKYO

Pergamon Flexible Learning
An imprint of Elsevier Science
Linacre House, Jordan Hill, Oxford OX2 8DP
200 Wheeler Road, Burlington, MA 01803

First published 1986
Second edition 1991
Third edition 1997
Fourth edition 2003

British Library Cataloguing in Publication Data
A catalogue record for this book is available from the British Library

ISBN 0 7506 5880 0

For information on Pergamon Flexible Learning
visit our website at www.bh.com/pergamonfl

Institute of Leadership & Management
registered office
1 Giltspur Street
London
EC1A 9DD
Telephone 020 7294 3053
www.i-l-m.com
ILM is part of the City & Guilds Group

The views expressed in this work are those of the authors and do
not necessarily reflect those of the Institute of Leadership &
Management or of the publisher

Authors: Clare Donnelly and Bob Foley
Editor: Clare Donnelly
Editorial management: Genesys, www.genesys-consultants.com
Based on previous material by Joe Johnson, Alastair Clelland and Raymond Taylor
Composition by Genesis Typesetting Limited, Rochester, Kent
Printed and bound in Great Britain by MPG Books, Bodmin

Workbook introduction

1 ILM Super Series study links

This workbook addresses the issues of *Budgeting for Better Performance*. Should you wish to extend your study to other Super Series workbooks covering related or different subject areas, you will find a comprehensive list at the back of this book.

2 Links to ILM qualifications

This workbook relates to the following learning outcomes in segments from the ILM Level 3 Introductory Certificate in First Line Management and the Level 3 Certificate in First Line Management.

C6.1 Performance Indicators
1 Identify means by which performance levels can be measured
2 Monitor performance against agreed targets
3 Make recommendations for improvement in performance or the adjustment to more realistic targets

C6.2 Working to a Budget
1 Explain the importance of operating within a budget
2 Monitor performance against budget

3 Links to S/NVQs in Management

This workbook relates to the following elements of the Management Standards which are used in S/NVQs in Management, as well as a range of other S/NVQs.

- A1.3   Make recommendations for improvements to work activities
- B1.1   Make recommendations for the use of resources
- B1.2   Contribute to the control of resources
- D1.1   Gather required information
- D1.2   Inform and advise others

It will also help you to develop the following Personal Competences:

- searching for information;
- thinking and taking decisions.

4 Workbook objectives

You will have plans for your career and your private life. There are things you will want to do today, tomorrow, next week, next year. And because most events and activities cost money, you will know that it's usually necessary to make financial plans to achieve your aims.

The same principles are relevant at work. Your organization has aims and objectives with financial implications and these are identified by using budgets.

By preparing budgets which allocate money to specific purposes, an organization seeks to gain more control over its activities. Careful monitoring then helps to ensure that spending is kept within bounds. Budgets are considered an essential tool by organizations in the management of their affairs.

As a first line manager, you are probably expected to meet budgetary targets, expressed in financial terms. But very detailed 'performance' targets are often much more practical, such as 'serve 20 customers per hour', or 'inspect five junction boxes per day'. This workbook is intended to help you understand how to meet performance targets, and agree targets that are realistic.

4.1 Objectives

When you have completed this workbook you will be better able to:

■ describe what a budget is;
■ understand how budgets are used;
■ use some budgetary control techniques;
■ identify ways of measuring performance levels;
■ describe a range of methods for measuring performance;
■ identify the differing objectives of stakeholders in the organization;
■ select the ideal performance measure;
■ monitor performance against agreed targets;
■ make recommendations for improvement in performance, or adjustments to more realistic targets.

5 Activity planner

The following Activities require some planning so you may want to look at these now.

■ Activity 7 – in which you look at budget deviations.
■ Activity 10 – which covers budget variances.
■ Activity 44 – where you use the balanced scorecard to suggest improvement.
■ Activity 48 – in which you gather information for measuring performance.
■ Activity 54 – which analyses the systems used, in order to improve work activities and control resources.

Some or all of these Activities may provide the basis of evidence for your S/NVQ portfolio. All portfolio activities and the Work-based assignment are sign posted with this icon.

The icon states the elements to which the portfolio activities and Work-based assignment relate.

The Work-based assignment, on page 101 suggests that you speak to your manager, finance director or to your colleagues in the accounts office about the way in which budgets are used in your organization. You might like to start thinking now about who to approach and arrange to speak with them.

Session A
What is a budget?

I Introduction

How would you feel if you were never sure if you would be paid on pay-day or not?

To ensure that you do get paid on the right day, your organization needs to plan and to control the ways in which it spends and receives money so that enough cash is available to pay wages and salaries when due. The organization draws up a plan indicating how it expects money to flow in and out. This plan is better known as a budget.

You probably do the same at home, planning how to use your income. You budget, your employer prepares a budget and, of course, the country as a whole budgets.

Each year, the Chancellor of the Exchequer presents a Budget to Parliament. Its aim is to achieve things which are part of the government's policy on how best to run the country.

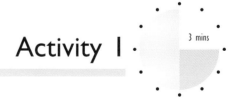

Activity I   3 mins

Write down three things the Chancellor might try to achieve through the annual Budget.

_____

_____

_____

Typical examples might be to:

- improve public services;
- reduce inflation;
- combat unemployment;
- help small businesses;
- win the next election!

Whatever plans and policies the government has, they all have to be financed. The Budget is all about getting hold of and using money.

To achieve this, the Chancellor might introduce policies to:

- cut or tighten control over major items of expenditure;
- switch expenditure and resources from one item to another;
- use a variety of financial incentives and penalties.

The national Budget requires a lot of analysis, planning negotiations and juggling with resources. It covers both national income and national expenditure. All budgets work in similar ways; just the amounts involved differ.

2 The purpose of budgets

Think about your own workplace for a moment. Your workteam may be earning income through the sales it achieves or the services it supplies.

Or it might be contributing to profit (the surplus of income over costs) in one or two other ways.

directly, by purchasing, manufacturing or processing materials, to produce goods that are sold	**indirectly**, by such things as designing, controlling, maintaining equipment, or providing services to customers or other workteams

Whatever it does, your workteam is certain to incur expenditure (costs), in doing its job. Almost certainly, the organization you belong to will have prepared a budget for its expenditure. If it generates income directly, then there will be a budget for that as well.

A budget can be described as:

a quantitative plan of action prepared in advance of a defined period of time.

Let's look at this definition more closely.

- **A budget is quantitative.**

  That means it must be stated in figures; in practice this usually means in sums of money. A general statement of what you intend to do may be useful, but it's not a budget.

- **A budget is prepared in advance.**

  A budget must be drawn up *before* the period to which it refers. Figures produced during or after the period may be important, but they are not part of a budget.

- **A budget relates to a particular period.**

  Budgets are drawn up for a certain specific period (often, though not always, one year). An open-ended financial plan for the future isn't a budget.

- **A budget is a plan of action.**

  This is perhaps the most important point of all. A budget can't be a definite statement of fact, because it relates to something which hasn't happened yet. It is what the organization is planning will happen.

Conditions may change during the budget period, which means the budget will be inaccurate. Like all plans, budgets seldom turn out to be totally correct predictions of the future. Even so, they can still be useful in guiding the actions of those using them. This guidance role is very important.

Of course, you must know what you are trying to achieve before planning. Everything else depends on that.

'Knowing what to achieve' is referred to in business as an **objective**.

The objectives of your workplace will depend to some extent on what kind of organization it is and may be short, medium or long term. Manufacturing industries, for example, have to make a profit. Local government services have to provide a certain level of service. A nationalized industry may be required to achieve a planned return on capital invested.

Some other examples of objectives are:

- to make a profit of 30% on a certain product;
- to increase the share of the market by 5% for a certain product;
- to improve service to the public in certain areas;

■ to survive commercially for a financial year (this is particularly relevant to new, small businesses).

To achieve any of these objectives needs planning and will probably involve the production of budgets.

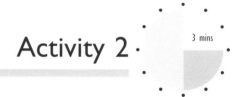

Activity 2

3 mins

Write down **two** different kinds of budget that are used in your organization to meet its objectives. One example would be a sales budget.

The budgets listed below are all common types. Perhaps your suggestions are among them, though you could well have thought of others too.

■ Sales budget.
■ Production budget.
■ Research and development budget.
■ Training budget.
■ Departmental costs budget.
■ Cash budget.

All budgets are important, although it is arguable that the cash budget is most important because without cash a business cannot survive.

Let's look briefly at sales budgets and cash budgets, to make sure we understand what they mean.

In a **sales budget**, a forecast is made of the sales the business will make during the relevant period. This may be broken down by section or department. Knowing how much you plan to sell is essential, in order to decide how much raw materials you will buy, how many employees you will need, and so on.

In a **cash budget** the business will forecast:

■ what cash will be received and paid out during the budget period;
■ the timing of receipts and payments;
■ the bank balance or overdraft for each month.

The cash budget is especially important for small, newly established businesses.

Activity 3

2 mins

Who do you think would need to see the cash budget of a newly established business? Write down **one** suggestion.

_____

_____

EXTENSION 1
Assignment 14 in *The Business Plan Workbook*, by C. Barrow, P. Barrow and R. Brown, gives illustrations of the situations faced by businesses that have and have not prepared a cash budget.

You may have thought of a number of possibilities. The one I had in mind was the bank manager who will want to examine the cash forecasts of a new business, and will almost certainly insist on a cash budget before authorizing a loan for a new business.

However, I don't want to give the impression that it is only new, small businesses which find cash budgets important. Organizations, large and small, use them, and so do charities and social clubs. Everyone needs cash.

3 Beginning a budget

The process of producing a set of budgets is covered in detail in the *Controlling Costs* workbook. Here, we are going to think about the beginning of the budget process. We'll start with manufacturing industry – in a business which makes and sells something.

We need first to identify the critical factor which influences all the budgets in a certain workplace. The factor influences all other budgets, and is called the **key** or **limiting budget factor**.

In practice:

■ the **sales budget** is the commonest limiting budget factor in established commercial businesses;
■ the **cash budget** is the commonest limiting budget factor in newly established small businesses.

Sometimes the **production budget** is the limiting budget factor, although this is less common.

In a non-profit organization, the limiting budget factor is likely to be the availability of funds.

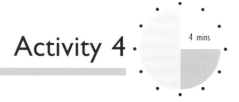

Activity 4

In each of the following situations, the key budget – the one on which other budgets will depend – will have to be produced first. To remind you, in a manufacturing company, this may be a **cash**, **sales** or **production** budget. Look at each situation and decide which is the key budget for each.

	Key Budget	
Firm A exists in a highly competitive market and currently sells 500 units per month. It plans to increase this to 600 units per month in the coming year and, in fact, has the capacity to produce 750 units per month.	Cash	☐
	Sales	☐
	Production	☐
Firm B is the sole supplier of a specialist component. It can sell all it produces and more.	Cash	☐
	Sales	☐
	Production	☐
Firm C is a small business with a large overdraft. It is currently owed a great deal of money, and its bank insists that the overdraft cannot be extended.	Cash	☐
	Sales	☐
	Production	☐
Firm D is a haulage contractor with a fleet of ten lorries on the road that has been offered a contract to transport 12 lorry-loads of goods to Southern Europe on a weekly basis. The firm cannot afford to purchase additional lorries.	Cash	☐
	Sales	☐
	Production	☐

Here is what I would say is the key budget, on which all other budgets would depend, for each of these firms.

- For Firm A, it's a sales budget. The firm must sell more. Everything else, including production, will follow from that.
- For Firm B, it's a production budget. The firm has to produce more. If it achieves this then extra sales will follow.
- For Firm C, it's a cash budget. The most important thing is for the firm to earn cash at the moment. This might even mean that the firm would have to refuse a potentially profitable contract if it didn't bring in cash quickly enough.
- For Firm D, the key is the cash budget because the firm does not have enough cash to buy more lorries to provide the transport service offered.

4 Why do we need budgets?

Some people think of a budget as something that restricts what we want or need to do. It certainly can be very frustrating when the constraints of a budget, drawn up by accountants who (you may feel) have no understanding of your problems, prevent you from taking certain actions in your job.

See if you recognize any of the following situations or something similar.

The training budget of a hospital has been spent. A nursing sister is refused permission to go on a course to learn how to use a new piece of equipment for monitoring heart disease. She is concerned because she feels that patient care may suffer.

The entertainments budget of a growing electronics firm is exhausted. The sales manager is unable to offer the kind of hospitality he would like to a visiting trade delegation from Saudi Arabia. No orders are won.

The overtime budget of a shipbuilding company is already overspent. No new overtime is authorized and the ship ends up three months late to the customer. Massive penalties result.

The departmental budget in the chemistry department of a university is underspent with one month of the financial year to go. The professor authorizes a spending spree to ensure his budget is not cut next year. Unneeded equipment which is rarely if ever used is purchased.

Having a plan, which is all the budget is, can only be a good thing. In these examples, the budgets themselves were not to blame for the unfortunate results. So what went wrong?

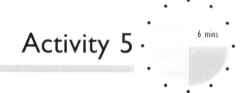

Activity 5 · 6 mins

Write down any ideas you have about who or what was responsible for the problems arising in any of the situations described above.

_____

_____

_____

_____

A budget is only a plan and provides guidance. Budgets should not be rigidly kept to as an excuse for not managing. Sometimes an adaptation of a plan is more sensible.

You may have noted a number of possibilities but perhaps we can narrow them down to the following.

■ An over-rigid view of how the budgets should be enforced has been taken – this seems likely to be the case in the first and second examples.
■ The budgets have been badly produced, managed and controlled, particularly the third and fourth examples.

If necessary, senior management usually have authority to over-ride a budget if they consider it would be economically worthwhile to do so. For example, it is probably appropriate to intervene to prevent the company having to pay contract penalties for late delivery, because its overtime budget is overspent. They might achieve this by transferring savings made in one budget to another, a process known as **virement**.

After all, budgets are intended to be beneficial.

It is when they are badly produced, managed and/or controlled, that they can have undesirable consequences.

But what do we mean by this? The easiest way to see how bad production, management and control of budgets have poor effects is to trace through the problems in one of the situations above.

Let's take a look at the hospital training budget example.

■ The training budget was drawn up at the beginning of the financial year without reference to the equipment budget, which showed that new equipment was being purchased to monitor heart disease.
■ BAD PRODUCTION – more access to information would have shown the need to budget for this training.

- Two key staff left and were not replaced. Instead a series of temporary staff, each of whom had to be trained in certain procedures, were taken on, so using up the training budget.
- BAD MANAGEMENT – more effort should have gone into recruiting permanent staff.
- A discretionary training course became available which had not been planned at the beginning of the year. All staff were ordered by the human resources department to go on the course, without evaluation of whether it was needed by the departments holding the training budget.
- BAD CONTROL – the usefulness of the training course in comparison with the heart disease monitor course should have been evaluated by the managers responsible for the heart disease ward.

Having seen the downside of poor practice, let us look at the benefits of good budget practice.

5 The advantages of budgets

Organizations benefit in a number of areas through budgeting.

- Co-ordination and teamwork

The process of budgeting means that management at all levels and in different departments are given the opportunity to meet, discuss and relate their targets to each other. Organizations are most successful if everyone works together to meet common goals rather than each manager acting selfishly to build their own empires.

The co-ordination process helps managers get an understanding of how each activity relates to the whole, which is very important for them and for the business. It would be pointless, for example, for the sales manager to plan a 10% increase if the production manager is aiming for a 5% cutback.

- Communication

In order to work to a budget, people have to **know** what is possible or impossible in their own workplace.

Budgeting encourages management at all levels to talk to one another about the company's policies and the targets they are aiming for. Again this builds teamwork; people working for each other and for their organizations.

■ Planning

As we've seen, planning is at the heart of a budgeting system. Using a budgeting system means that managers and supervisors have to use formal procedures to think about the future, instead of muddling along from one day to the next. It also means that thought is given to the level of performance expected in every part of the organization.

■ Control and performance evaluation

The whole point of a budget is to influence the direction the organization is taking. For a budget to be of value,

the actual outcome must be regularly compared with the planned outcome.

If the two don't match up, then controls can be used to take appropriate action. Without a plan there is no yardstick to measure what's happening; any controls, therefore, are fairly random.

The idea of a system of budgets is to get a clearer picture of planned activities and to make departments and individuals responsible for spending and cost control in their own areas. In this way, the strengths of sections and departments can be capitalized on, and ways found to overcome any weaknesses.

■ Motivation

The more people are involved at every level in setting up a budget, and in the planning and control that goes with it, the more they understand and support what the organization is trying to achieve. Involvement is an important motivating factor at any level.

All these points are valid, but the two most important purposes of budgets are **planning** and **control**. The planning process enables control to be exercised.

Let's explore the idea of budgetary control a little further.

6 Using budgetary control

Budgetary control involves drawing up budgets which relate what has to be done to the managers who have to do it, and then comparing actual results against the plan.

It is a very useful management tool. It should enable a manager or supervisor to do his or her job more effectively, without detracting from individual skill or flexibility.

Control must be an active process.

Activity 6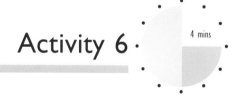

4 mins

Here is an important question for a manager, which budgets should help to provide the answer to. 'Is my workteam (or section, or department) keeping its spending within agreed limits?'

Can you think of at least **one** other question to which a manager might want to know the answer, and which budgets should help provide?

_____

_____

_____

You may have thought of several possible questions. Perhaps you included the following.

- 'Are we reaching agreed targets?'
- 'If we are not reaching agreed spending limits or agreed targets, where are we falling down, and for what reasons?'
- 'What can I do to try to improve the performance of my team?'
- 'Do events suggest that the budget needs to be modified?'

By monitoring actual results against budgets, control is improved. You should be able to identify problems and take action quickly, and there is less incentive just to let matters slide.

No budget is perfect. Unforeseen circumstances do arise. For example, a competitor may suddenly bring out a new product, the bottom may drop out of a market or we may have a strike on our hands. Any number of events can make budgeted figures less accurate, some within the control of managers, some not.

Activity 7 · 10 mins

S/NVQ B1.2

This Activity may provide the basis of appropriate evidence for your S/NVQ portfolio. If you are intending to take this course of action, it might be better to write your answers on separate sheets of paper.

Think about your own job.

Write down **two** factors that might make your workteam deviate from its budget, and which are largely **within** your control.

_____

_____

_____

_____

Now write down **two** factors that might make your workteam deviate from its budget, which are largely **outside** your control.

_____

_____

_____

_____

Your response will be related to your own job.

■   As factors within your control you might have put down answers such as faulty work, bad timekeeping by employees, inefficient organization of the department, new staff not inducted properly, and so on.

■ Factors likely to be outside a line manager's control are the hold-up of supplies, teething problems with new products or systems, shortages of staff and so forth.

Because there are many ways in which a budget can become out of line with the plan, an organization must try to obtain the best possible information at the time of preparing the budget. It should look to see, for instance, what it has achieved in the past, and what its costs actually are.

Self-assessment 1

10 mins

1 A properly drawn-up budget can be described as having **four** important features. Identify all four features.

_____

_____

_____

_____

2 Write down **two** initial uses for budgets at the time when they are drawn up.

_____

_____

_____

_____

3 Fill in the missing words in the following sentences.

a Budgets are largely a waste of time unless they are actively _____ in order to see whether the organization is_____ its targets and keeping within its limits.

b We use the term _____ _____ to cover the use of budgets to help an organization control its progress towards what it has set out to achieve.

c A budget will not be useful to an organization if it is managed so _____ that it does not permit some degree of flexibility.

Answers to these questions can be found on page 113.

7 Summary

- A budget is a **plan**, usually described in financial terms, prepared in advance of a defined period of time.

- The starting point in producing a budget is to determine the **key** or **limiting factor** which influences all other budgets. This will often be the sales budget.

- **Control** is central to the budgeting process. The system of using budgets and comparing actual and budgeted results to control progress towards stated objectives is **budgetary control**.

- Budgeting should never be so inflexible as to prevent sensible decisions being taken.

- Budgets can also help to improve:
  - co-ordination and teamwork;
  - communication;
  - motivation.

- Good budgeting should help an organization meet its goals and ensure that everyone works together towards those goals.

Session B
Monitoring performance against budget

1 Introduction

Producing a correct and realistic budget takes time. Putting the information together can take you away from your main job of producing or providing a service and make you ask yourself if budgeting is really worth all the expense and effort.

We have seen the benefits, but unless budgets really work they are not worth preparing.

In this session we look at several ways in which budgets are used, and what makes them important, especially in terms of planning and control.

As a first line manager you will be involved in implementing the budget allocation of your section or department in detail. You will monitor operations and ensure that your workteam works within budget as far as is possible, and will report on any differences from budget.

In this session you will see what costs you can control and which are uncontrollable. Knowing that will help you understand what actions you can take to make best use of the resources at your disposal and how to monitor those resources.

2 Budgetary control

All budgetary control systems follow basically the same steps:

EXTENSION 2
Further aspects of
budgetary control are
featured in *Budgeting for
Non-Financial Managers* by
Ian Maitland.

- establish agreed budgets;
- report actual results to departmental managers;
- identify where actual performance differs from planned performance (these differences are called **variances**);
- analyse which department and which manager is responsible for the variances;
- analyse why the variances have happened.

Activity 8

Acme Machine Tools Ltd prepared budgets for income from sales of machines (sales revenue) of £2,000,000 in the coming year. In the event, actual sales revenue turns out to be £1,750,000.

Identify **two** possible reasons why you think the variance (the difference between the planned and actual sales revenue) might have arisen, and who you think will be held accountable for the difference from the plan.

You may have thought of a number of possible reasons why the variance came about, but your suggestions can probably be grouped into these main areas:

- sales price per machine had to be lower than was forecast;
- the number of machines sold was fewer than forecast.

Of course, these problems would have to be investigated in more depth to find out what was causing them. It might be something like poor delivery dates, low quality or a competitor putting a better or cheaper product on the market.

As to who would be held accountable or responsible, it will be whoever was responsible for preparing the sales budget, whether that was the sales director, sales manager or whoever. This person may not be directly to blame for the variance, but he or she carries the responsibility for the problem.

Depending on the causes identified, the sales director will wish to discuss the issues with other managers. Poor delivery dates may be down to the distribution manager or the production director; low quality may also be part of the production director's remit, or that of the research and development director.

In order to monitor what is happening, managers need budgetary control reports to be sent to them periodically, highlighting variances for which they are responsible. Regular control is more likely to prevent major problems at the end of the budget period.

2.1 Reporting actual results and variances

Here is an extract from a budgetary control report for a manufacturing company.

	Budget	Actual	Variance	
Sales revenue	600,000	700,000	100,000	Favourable
Less costs:				
Materials in factory	250,000	280,000	30,000	Adverse
Wages in factory	100,000	120,000	20,000	Adverse
Machine running costs	45,000	50,000	5,000	Adverse
Salaries in administration	55,000	50,000	5,000	Favourable
General administration	20,000	15,000	5,000	Favourable
Advertising	15,000	20,000	5,000	Adverse
	485,000	535,000	50,000	Adverse
Operating profit	115,000	165,000	50,000	Favourable

As you can probably see from the figures above, a **favourable variance** indicates that:

- actual sales are greater than budgeted sales, or
- actual costs are lower than budgeted costs.

An **adverse variance** indicates that:

- actual sales are lower than budgeted sales, or
- actual costs are greater than budgeted costs.

In the example budgetary control report:

Sales – Costs = Operating profit.

You read just now that managers responsible for different budgets should periodically receive a budgetary control report, and should then be expected to explain variances. Usually senior management would be concerned with adverse variances of a certain size (some variance either way is almost inevitable), but favourable variances may also need investigation. This is because short cuts may have been taken to arrive at the apparent advantageous situation. Alternatively, managers may simply wish to learn from it for the future.

Activity 9 · 6 mins

Refer back to the budgetary control report for the manufacturing company, shown above.

Below is a list of the managers who receive a copy. Against each job title, state the variance which you think each of them would have to explain.

Purchasing manager (reports to factory manager)

_____

Factory manager

_____

Marketing manager

_____

You should have identified that the managers would have to explain the adverse variances as follows.

- Purchasing manager: materials in factory.
- Factory manager: materials and wages in factory, machine running costs.
- Marketing manager: advertising.

2.2 Why have the variances happened?

As we saw in the budget preparation statement, problems are likely to be interrelated, so that what happens in one area may be the result of a decision made in another area.

It is worth investigating the sales variance as something might be gained for other aspects of the business from the successes being achieved here. The same can also be said in the areas of salaries in administration and general administration, where the favourable variances are significant.

Managers may not always be able to take action about variances, whether favourable or adverse. This is because:

- some costs will be non-controllable;
- some costs may arise in the department but the responsibility may lie elsewhere. For example, time wasted in one department may be caused by the failure of another department to supply information or materials.

If you want to find out more about investigating the causes of variance, look at the *Controlling Costs* workbook.

Activity 10 · 15 mins

S/NVQs
B1.1, B1.2,
D1.1, D1.2

This Activity may provide the basis of appropriate evidence for your S/NVQ portfolio. If you are intending to take this course of action, it might be better to write your answers on separate sheets of paper.

Think about your own organization.

a To whom do you report variances from budgets and how quickly do you need to report?

_____

_____

_____

b   Who, if anyone, reports variances to you?

_____

_____

_____

_____

c   Why is it important for variances to be reported as required by your organization? How well are reports of variances followed up; are the causes always sought?

_____

_____

_____

_____

Your response will be related to your own job.

You are likely to report variances to your immediate line manager within a period depending on the significance of the variance. A major problem will require immediate reporting. In the same way, others may report to you.

The speed and extent of reporting depends on organizational policy and the trust you and your colleagues have in each other to deal with problems. You will presumably be able to take action on variances and take control of appropriate resources under your control, or make recommendations to your manager.

2.3   Non-controllable costs

Let's look a little more closely at what we mean by non-controllable costs. These are costs that are charged to a **budget centre**, the name given to a section of business on which a budget is built, such as sales or production, but which cannot be influenced by the actions of the people responsible for that budget centre.

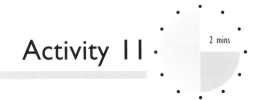

Activity 11

2 mins

Identify **one** example of what you think is a non-controllable cost that might be charged to the budget of your work area.

Here are some examples which came readily to my mind. I hope you can see that they are outside a manager's control.

■ A portion of the rates charged to a departmental budget for the premises it occupies.
■ Diesel fuel costs charged against the transport manager's budget where oil shortages cause prices to soar.
■ Heating costs in a work area where the heating system is controlled centrally.

Since these are outside the control of the manager concerned, it's important to identify them separately. Let's look at why this is important.

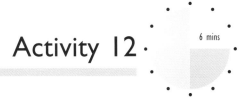

Activity 12

6 mins

Margaret Shaw is the manager of a school canteen with a monthly wages budget of £2,000. She receives a budgetary control report which tells her that the wages expenditure in her canteen for January, February and March has been £2,250 for each month.

Here are the reasons for overspending.

■ January: extra staff employed to cover sickness.
■ February: staff overtime to meet re-arranged schedules during annual school examinations.
■ March: implementation of a nationally agreed bonus scheme, which was not built into the budget.

We usually regard wages as a controllable cost. But is that entirely true in this case?

Decide whether the adverse variance in each month has been caused by controllable or non-controllable wages costs, and note briefly the reason for your decision.

	Controllable	Non-controllable	Reason
January	☐	☐	_____
February	☐	☐	_____
March	☐	☐	_____

Compare your answers with mine.

■ January's variance is **non-controllable**. A reasonable allowance for sickness should be built into the budget, but extra cost caused by excessive sickness could hardly be controlled by the manager.

■ February's cost, however, is **controllable**. The manager should have anticipated this problem. Overtime costs for predictable events would certainly be regarded as being within the manager's control.

■ March's extra costs are clearly **non-controllable**. National agreements lie outside the manager's control, and the budget will need to be adjusted to incorporate the extra payment.

We've said that it's important to discover who and what is responsible for any budget variance. This isn't a question of looking for someone to blame. The real issue is finding out why the variance has happened so that corrective action can be taken if necessary.

2.4 Causes of variances

At the beginning of this session we looked for reasons why there might be a variance on sales and decided that two of the likely causes are:

■ the quantity sold is different from the quantity budgeted (volume);
■ the selling price is different from the price budgeted (price).

Let's see how the variance on sales for the manufacturing company referred to on page 17 would be presented in the budgetary control report for the sales director. First we need a little more detail.

Remember that the company budgeted to make £600,000 in revenue and actually made £700,000. Why did this happen?

On investigation, we discover that the company budgeted to sell 50,000 units at £12 per unit, but actually sold 56,000 units at £12.50 per unit. How does this information help us?

We need to analyse the total sales variance into a volume variance (selling 6,000 more units than expected) and a price variance (selling units at 50p more than expected).

This can be presented as follows. (Don't worry too much about the maths at this point.)

	Budget	**Actual**	**Variance**
Sales volume	50,000 units	56,000 units	£72,000 Favourable
Selling price	£12.00	£12.50	£28,000 Favourable
Sales revenue	£600,000	£700,000	£100,000 Favourable

Having broken down the causes of the sales variance, the company needs to discover the underlying reasons.

Perhaps, in this case, the unit price was increased because another supplier went out of business and supplies were scarce, or because less discount was offered to customers. There could be all sorts of reasons.

We've seen that it's important to analyse sales variances by:

■ volume;
■ price.

We can analyse any variance on costs in a similar way.

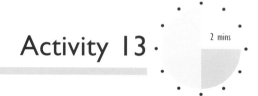

Activity 13 · 2 mins

Remember our manufacturing company has an adverse variance of £30,000 on the cost of materials in the factory. Jot down the **two** headings under which you think those cost variances could be analysed.

_____

_____

You may not have used the same words as I have but anything on similar lines is acceptable.

■ Volume

Did the business need more materials than budgeted to produce the units?

■ Expenditure

Did it have to pay more for the materials than budgeted?

All types of costs can be analysed in this way but we're just going to concentrate on two:

■ labour;
■ materials.

Activity 14 · 8 mins

A job is budgeted to take 50 hours and the labour per hour is £6·00. The actual hours taken are 55 and the hourly rate paid is £6·20.

Calculate the labour cost variance and suggest **two** reasons which you think might have caused the variances in time and the rate.

Budgeted cost = _____ × _____ = _____

Actual cost = _____ × _____ = _____

Variance = _____ (A/F)

Here are my calculations to compare with yours.

Budgeted cost = 50 × £6·00 = £300
Actual cost   = 55 × £6·20 = £341
Total variance = £41·00 (A)

We can break down the total variance like this.

- For the volume variance, calculate the number of excess hours worked (55 – 50 = 5) and multiply this number by the **budgeted** hourly rate of pay (£6).
- For the rate variance, calculate the difference between the actual rate paid and the budgeted rate (£6·20 – £6·00 = £0·20) and multiply this number by the **actual** hours paid (55).

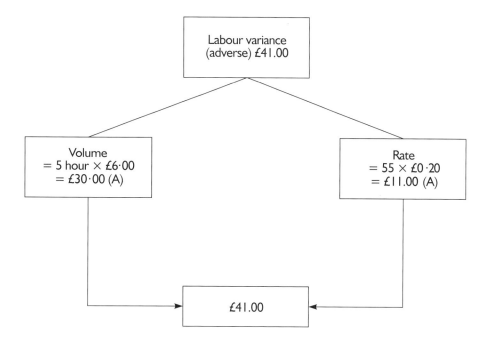

You may have suggested some of the following for the causes of the variances.

The volume variance might be caused by:

- slack work practices resulting from poor supervision;
- machine breakdowns;
- technical problems;
- bottle-necks, leading to material shortages.

The rate variance might be caused by:

- overtime or bonus payments
- unbudgeted pay award.

Now let's look at the cause of a total materials variance.

Activity 15

5 mins

A job is budgeted to use 1000 kilos of material at £3·00 per kilo.

The actual usage is 1200 kilos, but the price is £2·50 per kilo.

Calculate the total material cost variance, and analyse that into the price and expenditure variances. Write your answers on this diagram.

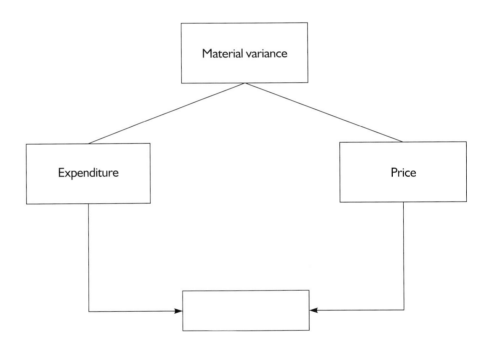

The answer to this Activity can be found on page 117.

3 Flexible budgets and budgetary control

In what we have said about budgetary control so far, we have assumed that we were using **fixed** budgets.

This means that, before the beginning of the period to which the budget relates, costs are budgeted for, and the budgeted costs remain the standard against which actual costs are compared, regardless of what happens during the budget period.

EXTENSION 3
Managing Budgets, a title in the Essential Managers series by Dorling Kindersley, describes the usefulness of using spreadsheets in budgeting. By using spreadsheets, a change in level of activity of, say, 5% can quickly and easily be made.

By using a **flexible budget**, on the other hand, we can make adjustments to costs if circumstances vary from the original budget.

A flexible budget is defined by the Chartered Institute of Management Accountants as:

'a budget which is designed to change in accordance with the level of activity attained'.

A flexible budget in fact consists of a series of budgets. Each one is based on a different level of sales or output. As an example, a company might budget for three possible levels of output; costs are then calculated for each level.

Despite the extra effort required in preparing these, flexible budgets can be very useful. Software packages certainly enable flexible budgets to be prepared easily and cheaply.

The first thing we have to do is to analyse costs into:

■ **fixed costs**, which *do not* vary with the level of production and sales;
■ **variable costs**, which *do* vary with production and sales.

Let's look at the difference this makes in practice.

We shall first assume that all costs are variable; that is, that they will vary in line with sales and production volumes. If we predict that production and sales will fall within the range of 2,000–3,000 units, we can work out the costs for both these figures.

Suppose each unit costs £5. Then the total costs for 2,000 units will be £10,000, and the total costs for 3,000 units will be £15,000.

The flexible budget would then look like this.

	Budget 1	**Budget 2**
Production/sales	2,000 units	3,000 units
Costs	£10,000	£15,000

In this case, the 2,000 units in Budget 1 is the lowest expected production/ sales figure; the 3,000 units in Budget 2 is the highest expected figure. The actual figures are expected to fall somewhere in between these two.

Say now that actual performance is to produce and sell 2,500 units. In the budgetary control report, since sales have turned out to be within the expected range, the budget figure written in for sales will be the same as the actual figure. The actual cost can then be compared with the expected costs for that figure. In the case above, the budgetary control report might appear as follows.

	Budget	**Actual**	**Variance**
Production/sales	2,500 units	2,500 units	
Costs	£12,500	£12,000	£500 (F)

Here the actual sales turned out to be 2,500 units (which is within the budgeted range), so the 'new' expected costs are 2,500 × £5 = £12,500. The actual costs were £500 less than this, so the variance is favourable.

Of course, not all costs are in practice variable; there are always some fixed costs.

Activity 16 ·

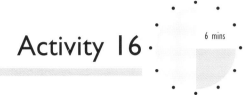

6 mins

Let's assume that we regard 50% of our costs as fixed and 50% as variable. The fixed costs are £5,000.

Complete the flexible budget and the budgetary control report in this instance.

Flexible budget

	Budget 1	Budget 2
Production/sales	2,000 units	3,000 units
Costs – fixed	£5,000	
– variable	£5,000	
Total costs		

Budgetary control report

	Budget	Actual	Variance
Production/sales	2,700 units	2,700 units	
Costs		£13,000	

As half the costs (£5,000) were fixed, they remain the same in Flexible Budget 2, even though sales are 1,000 more than in the first budget. But for Flexible Budget 2 we must calculate the expected variable costs for 3,000 units, as these do vary. We do this by working out the variable cost per unit from the first budget, and applying that to 3,000 units: £5,000/2,000 units = £2.50 per unit.

The variable costs for Flexible Budget 2 are then:

£2·50 × 3,000 units = £7,500.

So the total costs for Budget 2 are:

£5,000 fixed costs + £7,500 variable costs = £12,500.

The completed table is therefore as follows.

Flexible budget

	Budget 1	Budget 2
Production/sales	2,000 units	3,000 units
Costs – fixed	£5,000	£5,000
– variable	£5,000	£7,500
Total costs	£10,000	£12,500

Turning to the budgetary control report, the actual sales are 2,700 units and the actual costs are £13,000. We work out the flexible budget costs for 2,700 units as follows.

£5,000 fixed + (£2·50 × 2,700) = £11,750.

This gives an adverse variance of £1,250 (£13,000 − £11,750). So the completed table should look like this.

Budgetary control report

	Budget	Actual	Variance
Production/sales	2,700 units	2,700 units	
Costs	£11,750	£13,000	£1,250 (A)

3.1 The advantages of flexible budgets

Flexible budgeting is helpful to management in a wide variety of organizations where it is important to be able to take account of changes in circumstances.

Flexible budgets are particularly useful at:

- the planning stage;
- the end of the budget period, in order to revise figures to match reality and to plan for the future.

Using flexible budgets at the planning stage lets you consider the consequences of output being greater or less than expected, within a certain range.

So, if your planned output and sales are 10,000 units, flexible budgeting will allow you to consider in advance what will be the implications of achieving only 8,000, or what will be the opportunities of achieving 12,000 units.

Activity 17

5 mins

The outpatient department of a busy district hospital plans for 25,000 outpatient visits a year. Resources – doctors, nurses, secretarial back-up, waiting rooms, etc. – are geared to cope with 25,000 visits. Management use flexible budgeting to consider in advance the problems associated with there being 20,000 or 30,000 visits.

Identify **three** problems which might be anticipated if there are as many as 30,000 visits.

_____

_____

_____

The problems may appear endless. Among these are:

- failure to meet agreed service standards;
- over-tired doctors and other staff;
- overcrowding;
- increased litigation.

A flexible budget will show what the cost implications are across the board resulting from a change, so that managers can:

- think ahead;
- anticipate problems;
- arrive at possible solutions.

4 Non-financial budgets

Let's look briefly at non-financial budgets. All the budgets we've looked at so far have been concerned with money, but we can use the same techniques to help us plan for other key factors.

Here, for example, is how they can be used to provide information for management decisions on the allocation of resources in a hospital.

Medical specialism	Beds available	Occupancy (%)
Surgery	80	75
Medical	105	80
Geriatric	110	94
Maternity	38	89
Gynaecology	20	80

Now this may not appear like a budget, but the hospital managers are:

■ planning for bed usage;
■ recording their resources (beds);
■ recording the actual outcome (percentage occupancy);
■ presumably using the information for future plans.

Activity 18 · 2 mins

Take a look at the above table.

■ Which service is most efficiently managed?

_____

■ Which service may be worth reducing?

_____

Geriatric beds are occupied 94% of the time and are used very efficiently. Compared with this, surgery beds are only 75% occupied and this may indicate that the service could be reduced.

Of course, the 'beds available figure' is just the tip of the planning iceberg. Allocating new beds implies that more nursing staff, medical staff and back-up resources will need to be allocated to the specialist areas. Percentage occupancy figures do not indicate costs.

So, you can see the budget process can help manage in a wide range of areas; it need not be restricted to financial statements.

5 Standard costing and budgetary control

Standard costing is really a continuation of budgetary control. Let's see what it is and how it relates to budgetary control.

Here is how the Chartered Institute of Management Accountants defines standard cost.

'Standard cost is a predetermined calculation of how much costs should be under specified working conditions and standard costing is therefore a system which uses standards for costs (and revenue) to allow detailed control by the use of variances.'

Using standard costs enables us to work out what performance **should** be under certain conditions, so that we can identify variances and so control actual performance.

Perhaps this sounds rather similar to what we have already said about budgeting, particularly using fixed budgets.

Both standard costing and budgeting are:

- concerned with setting performance standards for the future;
- aids to control.

They are not, however, the same thing.

The important difference is that:

- budgets are concerned with totals – such as the costs of an entire department;
- standard costs are concerned with individual units; each item of production, for instance, will have a standard cost.

Activity 19

2 mins

If standard costing is concerned with individual units, do you think that this involves more or fewer people in budgetary control than in budgeting? Give reasons for your answer.

_____

_____

Standard costing takes budgetary control 'further down the line', and involves more people in having responsibility for meeting standards in their particular area of work. The advantages of having people involved are:

■ if unit costs are applied widely and lots of people are monitoring them, it is possible to identify variances on a much wider range of items, so improving control;

■ the setting of standards gives everybody a target to aim for and is likely to make more people cost conscious.

Self-assessment 2

20 mins

1 List **five** basic steps of budgetary control systems.

_____

_____

_____

_____

_____

2 State what is indicated by favourable and adverse variances.

_____

_____

_____

_____

3   Identify whether the following are controllable or non-controllable costs.

	Controllable	Non-controllable
a The produce purchased and sold by a greengrocer.	☐	☐
b The rent of a chair in a hairdressing salon.	☐	☐

4   Prizewinning Blooms expects to sell 100 bunches of red roses at £8·50 per bunch on Valentine's day. Sales are hit by a newspaper promotion of chocolates and the business is only able to sell 90 bunches by reducing them to £7·00 per bunch.

Calculate the total sales variance and indicate if it is favourable or adverse.

_____

_____

_____

5   Jack Simmons has received an estimate for painting a room of £320, being 16 hours at £20. As the painter was unable to complete the job and a less qualified person completed it, the actual cost was for 24 hours at £13 per hour.

Calculate the total labour cost variance and indicate if it is favourable or adverse.

_____

_____

_____

6   Briefly explain why flexible budgeting is useful to management.

_____

_____

7   A local theatre group has fixed costs of £200. It sells tickets for £5·00 each of which £3·00 is taken up by variable costs. How many tickets must the group sell to break even?

_____

_____

Answers to these questions can be found on page 114.

6 Summary

- Budgets must be put to use to achieve optimum results in organizations, in order to justify the time and effort involved in preparing them.

- Budgetary control allocates responsibility to managers who must achieve a plan, and allows for the identification and analysis of variances.

- Managers are held responsible for cost variances if these costs are within their control.

- Budgetary control can be achieved through fixed or flexible budgets, but flexible budgets are more useful.

- Non-financial budgets can provide management with useful information.

- Budgetary control is improved by a system of costing such as standard costing.

Session C
Measuring performance

1 Introduction

So far in this workbook we've been seeing how the things that first line managers and their workteams do can be monitored against an expected target called a 'budget'.

In this session we'll be taking a wider perspective, because budgets are not the only yardstick for measurement, and because first line managers are not the only people with a stake in the way an organization performs. So in this session we'll look at:

- a wide range of methods for measuring performance;
- how an organization's performance might be judged by the various people who have a stake in it.

2 What is performance measurement?

Suppose you run a 100-metre race in 15 seconds. How did you perform? There are lots of ways you could describe it (and you might be tempted to use the way that makes you look best when describing it to other people).

1 You could compare this performance to your previous attempts to run 100 metres. Were you faster or slower?

2 You could compare it to a target you have set for yourself, such as 100 metres in 12 seconds.

3 You could compare it to the times of other people in the race, or (if you are very ambitious!) to the world record time for running 100 metres.

All these descriptions are measurements of your performance. So let's have a definition.

Performance measurement considers how well something performs compared with how it performed in the past, or with how it is required to perform in the future, or in comparison with the performance of something else.

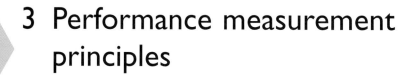

3 Performance measurement principles

In the 100-metre race we said you 'performed it' in 15 seconds, and 15 seconds is a sort of performance measurement. If you usually manage to run 100 metres in 13 seconds we might have said that your performance was 'below average'. If one person beat you in the race we could have said that you came 'second out of eight runners'.

'Below average' and 'second out of eight' are both performance measures.

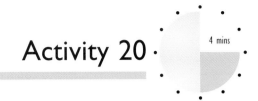

Activity 20

4 mins

For each of the three measures we used for your 100-metre race, what were you comparing your performance against? Which do you think is the most useful measure?

_____

_____

_____

_____

The first measurement is against the clock: it compares distance travelled with time taken. This is only useful if you happen to know other information, like how long it usually takes people of your age, sex and fitness to run 100 metres. The second is against your own previous performance, and that is useful information for you personally and for people who may compete against you in the near future. The third measurement compares you with other people.

Since I don't know anything else about you, I would say that the third measure is the most useful piece of information you could give me – but I would probably ask you who you were competing against.

The point is, the same performance can be presented in lots of different ways.

Activity 21

3 mins

Say you had to report your performance in the 100-metre race to your coach, your colleagues at work and your partner. Which measure would you use for each person?

1   Your coach _____

2   Your colleagues at work _____

3   Your partner _____

Probably it should be presented in the way that is most helpful to the person who wants the information, but very often information is presented in a way that makes the person presenting it look good.

3.1 Quantitative and qualitative measures

Information is quantitative if it can be expressed in numbers (or 'quantities'). 'Five apples' or '2 kg of apples' or 'a bag of apples costing £1.50' are all examples of quantitative information.

Information is qualitative if it is not expressed in numerical terms (for instance 'below average'), either because it can't be, or because it can't be in a way that has an agreed meaning.

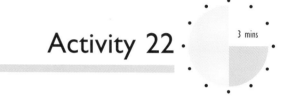

Activity 22

3 mins

Describe 'very delicious apples' as fully as you can.

_____

_____

_____

_____

If you need to describe the quality of something, it's generally more helpful to give as much detail as possible. This at least gives someone a chance to judge the apples in comparison to things they know about.

You may argue that 'very delicious apples' could be expressed numerically. You could say 'apples to which I would give a deliciousness rating of 10 out of 10'. But different people have very different ideas about what they think is a delicious apple. How do you judge?

Activity 23

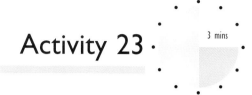

3 mins

If you had to choose between the two performance measures for apples below, which would you choose and why?

1   These apples are green, crisp, hard, juicy and sharp on the tongue.

2   I give these apples a deliciousness rating of 5 out of 10, and so do my three colleagues.

I hope you agree that quantitative information (description 2) is the most useful for performance measurement. (This does not mean that qualitative information should never be used, especially if there is a way to express it in a mixture of quantitative (objective) terms and qualitative (subjective) terms.)

If you had bought that bag of apples that rated 5 out of 10, and you wanted to increase your colleagues' apple-eating pleasure, the numbers give you a very clear target to beat: you just have to shop around for apples that rate more highly.

In addition, by saying '. . . and so do my three colleagues', the second measure is much more convincing than the first, purely personal opinion.

Activity 24

3 mins

In a supermarket you notice that the label on one of the bottles of organic apple juice you are thinking of buying has 'Silver Award Winner' printed on it. Is this an example of performance measurement? If so, why?

Look back at the definition of performance measurement at the beginning of this session if you are not sure.

_____

_____

_____

The award implies that the apple juice performed well enough to come second overall in an organic apple juice competition (presumably judged by experts) in comparison with other juices, so yes it is certainly a performance measure.

Watch out for other examples of attempts to 'quantify' qualitative measures. It is a common technique in advertising.

3.2 Comparing numbers: percentages

In this workbook we've already compared actual performance with budgeted performance, by subtracting one number from the other and calling the difference a variance.

There are other ways of looking at numbers in organizations. The most common way in performance measurement is the percentage.

Activity 25 · ⊙ 5 mins

Jumbo Ltd manufactures pet products. It had sales of £23,500 in January, £19,900 in February and £27,400 in March. By how much did sales fall in February and rise in March? Express you answer as a percentage to two decimal places.

_____

_____

_____

_____

In February, sales fell by £(23,500 − 19,900) = £3,600. To express this as a percentage, you divide the difference between the two numbers by the earliest number, and multiply by 100: £(3,600/23,500) × 100% = 15.32%.

In March sales rose (compared with February, the earliest number) by £(27,400 − 19,900) = £7,500, or £7,500/£19,900 × 100% = 37.69%.

Another way of looking at this is simply to divide one number by the other. For instance you could say that February sales are only 84.68% (£19,900/£23,500) of January sales, while March saw sales of 137.69% of February sales. (Remember: it is the thing that the percentage is 'of' that represents 100%.)

	£	%		£	%
February	19,900	84.68	**February**	19,900	**100.00**
Decrease	3,600	15.32	Increase	7,500	37.69
January	23,500	**100.00**	March	27,400	137.69

Here are a few examples of how percentages are used in performance measurement.

■ **Market share**
A company may set a target of 25% share of the total market for its product. The marketing department's performance will be measured on the difference between this and the actual market share achieved.

■ **Capacity levels**
'The factory is working at 15% below full capacity' is an example suggesting that the factory is not producing as much as it could, perhaps because of inefficiencies.

■ **Staff turnover**
If a department has staff turnover of 15% over a year, when the average in the organization is only 5%, there may be some problem in the way that department is performing.

3.3 Comparing like with like

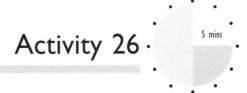

Activity 26 · 5 mins

We have the following additional information about Jumbo Ltd.

Sales	2003	2004
January	23,500	34,200
February	19,900	28,900
March	27,400	48,200

Can you see a pattern here? Describe them below, as fully as you can. What reasons can you think of for the pattern?

_____

_____

_____

_____

_____

_____

You should be able to see a pattern: sales fall in February and rise in March in both years. There could be a number of reasons for this: perhaps the January figures are boosted by post-Christmas sales, February is about normal and March is the time when the company releases its new Spring range of products.

In a case like this, it is not particularly useful to compare a month with the month before, since we already know roughly how sales will rise and fall between January and March. It is not really fair to compare March sales (the new product range) with February sales (the end of the old product range): we are not comparing like with like.

A better way of measuring would be to compare sales in 2004 with sales in 2003.

Sales	2003	2004	Increase
January	23,500	34,200	45.53%
February	19,900	28,900	45.23%
March	27,400	48,200	75.91%

Here we can see that in both January and February, sales are about 45% higher than they were in the previous year. But in March, sales are 75% higher than last year: the Spring 2004 product range has been much more successful on its launch than the Spring 2003 range was when it was first introduced.

If you get unexpected results you should always check that the principle of comparing like with like is being applied.

Just think of the 100-metre race: if all the other competitors were 30 years older than you, your work colleagues might not be quite so impressed that you came second!

Activity 27 ·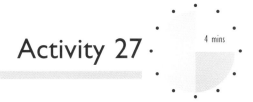

4 mins

Company A made a profit in the year to 31 December 2003 of £73,900. In the same period, Company B made a profit of £82,500.

What other information would you need to compare the performance of these two companies?

_____

_____

_____

_____

_____

On the face of it, Company B did a bit better than Company A, but we have no idea whether we are comparing like with like.

If Company A's sales were £100,000 and Company B's sales were £500,000, then Company A was actually a lot more successful. We can see this by calculating the profit margin – profit divided by sales – and comparing these.

	Profit (£)	Sales (£)	Profit margin
Company A	73,900	100,000	73.9%
Company B	82,500	500,000	16.5%

It would also be useful to know what the two companies actually do. Company A might be a firm of solicitors while Company B might make bathroom accessories, in which case there is little point in comparing their performance.

More information about costs would be helpful. Perhaps Company B had unusually large expenses during the year that will not recur in subsequent years.

And it would be helpful to know how much profit the companies made in previous years.

4 A range of performance measures

In most business organizations, popular ways of measuring performance are profitability, activity and productivity.

■ **Profitability**
Profit is made up costs and income. All parts of an organization incur costs, and so everyone's performance can be judged in relation to cost. Only some parts of an organization receive income, and their success should be judged in terms of both cost and income.

■ **Activity**
All parts of an organization carry out activities. An example of an activity measure is 'Number of orders received from customers'. This is a measure of the effectiveness of the marketing department. Activities can be measured in terms of physical numbers, monetary value, or time spent.

■ **Productivity**
This is the quantity of the product or service produced in relation to the resources put in, for example so many units produced per hour, or per employee, or per tonne of material. These are measures of efficiency.

Activity 28

2 mins

Circuit Ltd makes circuit boards for the electronics industry. Its production department has two production targets. Identify which is an activity target, and which is a productivity target.

1 At least 15 batches of circuit boards should be produced each week.

  Activity target ☐   **Productivity target** ☐

2 At least 1,000 circuit boards should be produced per hour of production time.

  Activity target ☐   **Productivity target** ☐

Circuit Ltd produces circuit boards in batches, and in one week it can produce at least 15 batches. We don't know how many boards there are in each batch, nor how many resources are used in a week, so Target 1 is an activity target. Target 2 measures both factory time and the number of circuit boards produced, so this is a productivity target.

5 Financial performance measures

Financial measures are calculated using figures in the organization's accounting records. Financial measures only tell us something about whether performance is good or bad because they are **compared** with something else.

Activity 29 ·

Here are some examples of financial performance measures, accompanied by comments that you might typically read in the financial pages of a newspaper (these are derived from the *Financial Times*).

For each one, try to identify what the performance is being compared with, and what the comparison shows.

■ Profit: 'the company made pre-tax profits in 2002 of £1.46m (2001: £1m) on sales of £12.7m (2001: £10.7m)'.

■ Sales: 'the aluminium division had sales which accounted for approximately 10% of the group's total sales'.

■ Costs: 'savings from the cost-reduction programme were £30m a quarter'.

■ Share price: 'the group's share price rose 15p to 684p despite the stock market's overall fall'.

You may have expressed your ideas differently but see how they compare with mine.

■ This year's profits and sales are compared with last year's, and are found to be higher.
■ Sales for one part of the organization are compared with the total for the group. The comparison shows a certain level of sales, but does not indicate whether this is an improvement or a deterioration.
■ Costs are compared with a previous period. They are at a lower level, in keeping with a planned reduction.
■ Share price is higher than before and high relative to the performance of the stock market as a whole.

Here is a list of yard-sticks against which figures in an organization's accounts are usually placed so that they become measures.

■ Budgeted sales, costs and profits, or standards in a standard costing system.
■ The trend over time (comparing last year to this year, say).

- The results of other departments of the organization.
- The results of other organizationes, especially competitors.
- The market in general.
- The economy in general.
- The organization's future potential (for example a promising new organization may make large losses in its first few years, but its performance should be judged in terms of how long it will be before it starts to make large profits).

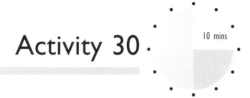

Activity 30 · 10 mins

See if you can get hold of a copy of your own organization's latest Annual Report and Accounts and glance through it to see what sort of financial performance measures you can spot.

If you've studied any accounting you'll know that there are several ratios that can be calculated to show how an organization is performing. Examples are the current ratio, profit margin and return on capital employed.
Another workbook in this series, *Understanding Finance*, tells you about financial ratios in more detail.

I logged on to the Internet and tapped 'Annual Report and Accounts' into a search engine.

The first thing I found was the Annual Report and Accounts of Unilever, which has a liberal sprinkling of financial performance measures just in the first few pages. Examples I found were: 'Leading brands account for 84% of total sales . . .', 'In Africa, Middle East and Turkey, overall sales were up by 2%, with profits increasing by 13%' and many others.

6 Non-financial performance measures

Financial measures do not necessarily give the full picture of an organization's performance, and in any case as a first line manager you may not have access to many accounting figures for your section or department.

49

Activity 31 ·

3 mins

What measures would you prefer to see for judging your workteam's performance? Does the accounting system measure these?

_____

_____

_____

_____

_____

Your team may be best judged by looking at units produced, time taken, product quality, delivery, after-sales service or customer satisfaction, none of which is directly measured by the traditional accounting system.

Unlike traditional variance reports, non-financial indicators are more relevant for non-financial managers, who can understand and therefore use them more effectively.

We can supplement financial measures in each of the following key areas of an organization:

- sales-related activities;
- materials;
- labour.

6.1 Sales-related activities

Traditionally, sales performance is measured in terms of price and volume variances, but other possible measures include revenue targets and target market share. You can analyse these measures in as much detail as you like: by country or by region, by individual products, by salesperson and so on.

Example of a financial measure.

- *Sales are up by 14%.*

Examples of non-financial measures.

- **Goods returned: total sales**
  '0.5% of goods were returned by customers.'
  This helps you to monitor customer satisfaction, and is a check on whether quality control procedures are working

■ **Deliveries late: deliveries on schedule**
'12% late deliveries.'
This comparison can be applied both to sales made to customers and to receipts from suppliers, and measures the efficiency of the stores department

■ **Number of people served and speed of service**
'100 people served in one hour.'
In a shop, if it takes too long to reach the checkout point, customers will go elsewhere and future sales will be lost.

■ **Customer profitability analysis**
'An average of £100 profit was made per customer.'
This measure may not be so useful, as profitability can vary widely between different customers. Different customers may be given different levels of discount, delivery costs are higher the further away the customer is, some customers demand more support than others, and so on. Information on this can help you check whether individual customers are actually profitable to sell to, and whether profitability can be improved for any customer by switching effort from one type of activity to another.

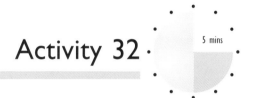

Activity 32

5 mins

A motor insurance company has collected the following data about claims on its insurance policies in the last year.

Age group	Number of policies	Total premiums (£)	Total claims (£)	Profit or loss (£)
18–25	2,700	837,000	855,000	
25–35	3,400	1,003,000	520,000	
35–50	5,400	1,350,000	120,000	
50–65	3,400	765,000	20,000	
Over 65	1,000	305,000	300,000	

Which group of customers is the most profitable for the insurance company and which is the least profitable?

Subtract the total claims from the total premiums per group to give you the profit per group. (You can also divide the profit per group by the number of policies to find out the average profit per person.)

	Total premiums (£)	Total claims (£)	Profit or loss (£)	Profit or loss per policy (£)
18–25	837,000	855,000	−18,000	−6.67
25–35	1,003,000	520,000	483,000	142.06
35–50	1,350,000	120,000	1,230,000	227.78
50–65	765,000	20,000	745,000	219.18
Over 65	305,000	300,000	5,000	5.00

The 18 to 25 age group is the only one that is not profitable, and the 35 to 50 age group is most profitable.

You might think that the company should stop selling insurance policies to 18 to 25 year olds – but they will of course get older and become more responsible drivers. The company will want to keep them as customers in the future.

What about the tiny profit made on policies sold to those aged over 65? This is probably a lot of work for little income, and the company might consider either raising the premiums or stop selling insurance to people over 65.

6.2 Materials

Traditional measures for materials are standard costs, and price and usage variances. Again there are many non-financial measures that can be helpful.

- **General physical quality**
  This will be important to the final product. Materials may have to have smoothness, or hardness, or pliability, or consistency of colour or taste
- **Particular physical quality**
  The material may need to be perfectly round or weigh a specific amount. Nothing less than 100% performance will do.

Activity 33

4 mins

You are a first line production manager working in a perfume bottling factory. You are responsible for manufacturing the stoppers for the tops of the bottles, and your colleague is responsible for ensuring that the perfume is not contaminated by other smells as it is bottled.

What non-financial performance measures could you expect to see for each process?

_____

_____

_____

_____

_____

_____

Measures in such cases can be expressed in terms of number of defects: '2 out of every 100 stoppers produced had the hole in the wrong position'; '6 out of every 10,000 bottles of perfume failed the 'sniffer' test'.

The performance of materials suppliers should also be measured: how quickly they deliver materials, whether they are ever late with their deliveries, and how many of the items they deliver are sent back because they are faulty.

6.3 Labour

Labour costs are traditionally measured in terms of rate and volume variances.

Other staff-related measures are possible, such as:

- unit sales per salesperson;
- time taken to do a task;
- hours lost through sickness.

Almost any aspect of an organization can be measured in terms of the different individuals or teams who carry out activities.

Qualitative measures concentrate on things like:

- ability to communicate;
- relationships with colleagues;
- customers' impressions ('so and so was extremely helpful/rude');
- levels of skills attained.

Employee-based measures are very important when assessing the performance of the employees' manager, as well as the employee. High profitability or tight cost control should not be accompanied by 100% staff turnover!

Activity 34

5 mins

John works in the Claims Processing Department of an insurance company with 14 colleagues. They are all paid £18,200 per annum and work a 7-hour day, 5 days a week. The department typically handles 1,500 claims each week of the year.

The department's manager wants to measure the performance of the department. Identify as many useful performance measures as you can think of, explaining what each is intended to measure and how it is calculated.

One morning John spends half an hour on the phone to his sister, who lives in Australia, at the company's expense. The cost of the call proves to be £16. What is the cost of John's half hour of idle time?

Here are some suggestions for measures, with explanations of how they are calculated.

- Claims processed per employee per week: 1,500/15 = 100 (activity measure).
- Staff cost per claim: (£18,200 × 15)/(1,500 × 52) = £3.50 (profitability).
- Claims processed per department hour: 1,500/(7 × 5) = 42.9 (productivity).
- Cost of John's half hour of idle time: £16 + £5 = £21 (profitability) John earns £10 per hour: £18,200/(7 × 5 × 52).

You may have thought of other measures and probably have slight rounding differences.

6.4 Dangers of non-financial measures

If you have too many measures you will be overloaded with information and may not be able to act on any of it properly.

Non-financial measures might lead managers to pursue detailed goals for their own departments, and lose sight of the goals for the organization as a whole.

7 External comparisons

Suppose you read in the newspaper that 'X plc made a profit of £3m, as opposed to £7m last year'.

On the face of it, it looks as if X plc has not done very well this year. But you should be well aware by now that it is not fair to pass judgement without comparing X plc's performance with something else.

7.1 The state of the economy

Economic influences should be considered whenever an organization's performance is measured.

What factors in the economy as a whole would you consider if you were assessing the performance of X plc, a retailer?

_____

_____

_____

_____

You may have questioned whether the economy is booming or in recession. Is the government trying to encourage organization growth, control inflation, reduce unemployment, or balance imports and exports?

Economic factors like these will affect interest rates and taxation, foreign exchange rates, the availability of skilled staff, and – crucially for X plc – the willingness of customers to spend money. All these things will have an impact on X plc's performance.

7.2 Competitors

You can compare the performances of different business organizations by calculating the same financial measures for each one, using published accounts, to see whose are better and whose are worse than average.

You can also get information about competitors through:

- newspaper and magazine reports and articles;
- their promotional material, advertising, website and so on;
- market research;
- recruiting ex-employees of rival organizations.

Activity 36

8 mins

Find out the following economic figures. You could look in a broadsheet newspaper such as *The Times*, or search the Internet (for instance http://www.statistics.gov.uk/ is a good source).

Rate of inflation _____   Bank base lending rate _____

Exchange rates: pound sterling/US dollar _____ pound sterling/euro _____

Rates of corporation tax _____

We won't give answers, because all these figures are likely to have changed by the time you read this. Hopefully, in the course of your research you will also come across other economic statistics that are relevant to your own organization's industry.

7.3 Benchmarking

Benchmarking analyses the performance of your own organization, or part of it, compared with the performance of another organization or part, which is generally regarded as 'the best' at the activity in question.

There are several types of benchmarking.

- **Competitor benchmarking** looks at direct competitors using any available published information, plus information from customer and supplier interviews.
- **Process benchmarking** looks at similar 'processes' in different organizations. For example, British Airways learned lessons about how to maintain their aircraft in foreign airports by looking at processes in organizations that maintain photocopiers.
- **Internal benchmarking** looks at different parts of the same organization, such as the security measures taken in different branches of the same shop to see which approach is most effective at preventing shop-lifting.

Activity 37 · 3 mins

What do you think are the advantages of benchmarking? Can you see any disadvantages?

Benchmarking is a good way of avoiding complacency, and it can give rise to new ideas. Also, staff are more likely to accept that they are not being asked to perform miracles if they can actually see new methods working in another organization.

But you probably spotted that persuading other organizations to share information may be a problem. Direct competitors won't want to give away their secrets or reveal their weaknesses. Worse, they may provide false information.

And processes can't always be transferred successfully. A way of working that succeeds in one organization may not work at all in another organization, especially if it depends on the talents of particular individuals.

8 Stakeholders and their objectives

Different people are interested in different aspects of performance, so it is measured in lots of different ways. For every organization there are individuals, groups of people, and other organizations, each of whom has an interest (a 'stake') in how the organization performs.

These people are called **stakeholders**, and there are three main types.

- **Internal stakeholders**: employees, at all levels.
- **Connected stakeholders:** owners; shareholders; members or subscribers of the organization; customers; financiers (banks, venture capitalists and the like); suppliers and partners.
- **External stakeholders**: the general community, local and central government, pressure groups and professional or industry bodies.

Activity 38

2 mins

Who else might have an interest (or a 'stake') in your performance in the 100-metre race?

_____

_____

_____

If I ran in this race I have to admit that my doctor would probably be rather concerned, and would be standing by with a resuscitator! Hopefully you had lots of better ideas.

- Other people in your race would be interested, and competitors in other heats.
- Your team-mates taking part in other events would want you to win points for the team.
- The race officials would be concerned that the race was conducted fairly.
- The audience would probably have favourites: they may even have placed bets on how well you will do.

8.1 Internal stakeholders

Everyone who works for the organization, from the most junior new recruit to the senior managers, is an internal stakeholder.

They have a personal stake in the organization's continued existence, because it is a place where they spend a great deal of their time and energy, and it pays their wages or salaries.

Employees also have more specific individual interests and goals. Here are some typical examples.

■ A secure income, and probably increases in income over time.
■ Career development.
■ Human contact and a sense of belonging to a team.
■ Interesting work that offers opportunities to use and develop skills.
■ A safe and pleasant working environment.
■ A sense of doing something worthwhile.

Activity 39

3 mins

Suppose your organization has announced that it is about to make some staff redundant, and jobs in your department are at risk. How might individuals' personal objectives affect their performance and so the overall performance of the department?

_____

_____

_____

_____

I would say the answer depends on what each person's main objectives are, whether they like their job, what their other prospects are, and what they stand to gain or lose from being made redundant.

Staff members who don't like their job much may well let their performance drop off. And if they stand to receive a generous enough redundancy package to leave them financially secure until they find another job, they won't make any special effort for the organization.

Staff whose prospects elsewhere are bad, or who are very keen to stay on because of personal objectives will probably perform extra well, to make it clear to managers that they are indispensable.

8.2 Connected stakeholders

Connected stakeholders include the following.

■ **Owners, shareholders, members or subscribers**
Their objective is to get a return on the money (or time, if it is a club) they have invested in the organization. If they did not invest their money, the organization would not exist at all, so earning a return is usually a commercial organization's prime objective.

■ **Customers**
They want products and services that meet their needs. They are interested in quality, price and dependability of supply. Customers can be very powerful (for instance, Sainsbury's is a much bigger organization than most of the ones it buys from) and have a huge effect on prices and procedures. Individual customers may band together into user groups with a strong interest in performance. Customers of rail and bus services are good examples.

■ **Financiers**
They want to know that any loan or overdraft they make, and the interest on it, will be repaid.

■ **Suppliers and partners**
They expect to be paid, so they have a stake in the organization's financial stability. They will also be keen to do future business, so it is in their interests that the organization survives and grows.

Activity 40   3 mins

Suppliers are sometimes regarded as 'the enemy'. Purchasing departments seek out the lowest-price suppliers and constantly switch supply sources to avoid getting too dependent on any individual supplier. Supplier contracts feature heavy penalty clauses and are drawn up in a spirit of general mistrust of all external providers. Information is deliberately withheld in case the supplier uses it to gain power during price negotiations.

What are the disadvantages of treating suppliers in this way?

_____

_____

_____

_____

_____

If you always pay late, or disrupt suppliers' plans by placing impossible demands upon them, or switch contracts, eventually no supplier will want to do business with you.

But there is a bigger disadvantage: the supplier's knowledge and skills are not exploited effectively. You buy products and services from suppliers because they are better at providing them than you are. The more they know about your product, your customers' needs, and your plans for the future, the better able they will be to provide you with the supplies you need.

Forward-thinking organizations recognize this and enter into partnerships with key suppliers. They open up their design departments and share their supply problems, and this helps generate new ideas, solutions, and products.

It may well be in your interest to share information with suppliers. This applies within organizations, too: if your workteam is dependent on another to supply materials or information, it is in your interest to collaborate with the other workteam as much as possible.

8.3 External stakeholders

External stakeholders are varied and have very varied objectives. Here are some examples.

- **The general community**
  This is interested because organizations bring local employment and facilities (shops, restaurants), and national benefits such as exports and know-how. They can also affect the natural environment, for instance by increasing road traffic, polluting water or air, or making excessive noise.
- **Local and central government**
  They are interested in tax revenue, compliance with laws that are meant to benefit everyone, such as the Health and Safety at Work Act, and employment prospects.
- **Pressure groups**
  They have particular interest in certain aspects of the organization's activities. For example, animal rights activists may object to an organization's methods of testing products.
- **Professional or industry bodies**
  They seek to develop 'best practice' standards and defend their members' interests where there is possible conflict with other external stakeholders. They also ensure that members' activities don't bring the profession or industry into disrepute.

Activity 41

What aspects of your organization's performance would a trade union be interested in?

_____

_____

_____

_____

_____

_____

You may have some ideas that are specific to your organization, but here are some general suggestions.

■ Rates of pay, and pay rises, relative to other equivalent organizations.
■ Statistics about recruitment policy, particularly with regard to ethnic and minority groups.
■ Workers' rights and working conditions.
■ Output and productivity information, since this is relevant to job security and the fairness of rates of pay.

8.4 Differing objectives

The objectives of all these different stakeholders can be sharply in conflict.

Activity 42 ·

Company A has made a large profit in the last financial year, and its shareholders and bank are very pleased. Why might the stakeholders below be less satisfied?

Internal stakeholders

_____

_____

Customers

_____

_____

The community

_____

_____

Suppliers

_____

_____

In a situation like this you have to put yourself in the shoes of the other stakeholders. How did the company make its profits?

- It might pay very low wages or expect staff to work impossibly long hours.
- Corners might have been cut, with an adverse effect on the quality of the product.
- No money may have been spent on local community projects.
- No money may have been spent developing innovative new products.

I hope you can see that different information is useful depending on what your stake in the organization is and what you want to know about it.

Many organizations have developed performance measurement systems to report on a variety of aspects of performance and reflect the interests of all stakeholders. Let's look at one of the best-known modern approaches, the balanced scorecard.

8.5 The balanced scorecard

This looks at an organization from four different points of view.

Perspective	Question	Areas of concern and examples of performance targets
Customer	What do existing and new customers value from us?	Cost, quality, delivery etc. 'Deliver within two working days'
Internal	What processes must we excel at to achieve our financial and customer objectives?	Internal ways of doing things and decision making 'Minimize stock holding costs'
Innovation and learning	Can we continue to improve and create future value?	Ability to acquire new skills and develop new products 'Sales of new products to be 20% of sales of existing ones' 'Minimize time to market for new products' 'Increase spend on training by 10%'.
Financial	How do we create value for our shareholders?	Ability to increase return to shareholders 'Widen profit margins by 2%'

EXTENSION 4
If you want to find out more about implementing this very useful technique, try following the guidance in *Balanced Scorecard Step-by-Step: Maximizing Performance and Maintaining Results* by P. R. Niven and R. S. Kaplan.

You can see that answers to the questions help identify areas for improvement. Appropriate performance targets (both financial and non-financial) can then be set.

For instance if the answer to the question 'What do customers value?' is 'fast delivery', then specific targets can be set ('Deliver within two working days'). Internal processes that aim to ensure delivery in two days can be set up, and performance can be monitored to see whether the target is being met.

A 'process' is simply a way of doing something. If you run out of a certain raw material, for example, there will be a 'process' for getting new supplies, such as: 'Write out a stock requisition, get it authorized by the project manager, send it to the purchasing department, identify the best supplier, place an order, take delivery and check for quality, accept delivery into stores'. The target might be to maintain a minimum level of stock and to avoid going out of stock of any item.

The scorecard is balanced because managers are expected to take account of all four perspectives when they look at performance. This should prevent improvements being made in one area at the expense of others.

Activity 43

6 mins

A company develops a new car with indicators that get louder as the car goes faster, so that they are not accidentally left flashing when driving at high speed on a motorway. The company has the processes and technology to make such a device at a reasonable cost.

Use the balanced scorecard to see whether this is a good idea.

Perspective	Question	Evaluation
Customer	What do existing and new customers value from us?	
Internal	What processes must we excel at to achieve our financial and customer objectives?	
Innovation and learning	Can we continue to improve and create future value?	
Financial	How do we create value for our shareholders?	

At first this sounds like a good innovation in response to a specific customer need. Certainly the evaluation of the internal, innovation/learning and financial perspectives would be positive.

But if you think about it a little more deeply, it may be that the customer perspective is wrong – that what the customer really wants is a better sound-proofed car with a quieter engine, not an even noisier car!

This is an example of focusing too much on innovation without thinking through what the customer really values.

Activity 44

S/NVQ A1.3

This activity may provide the basis of appropriate evidence for your S/NVQ portfolio. If you are intending to take this course of action it might be better to write your answers on separate sheets of paper.

Draw up a balanced scorecard for your part of your organization, and aim to include at least three performance measures under each heading.

You will need to begin by identifying the stakeholders in your part of the organization and determining what their interests are. Remember that other departments are 'customers' of your department, and your department has its own internal suppliers.

The financial perspective can include budget targets if this is most appropriate.

Looking at the completed scorecard, what ideas for improvements does it suggest?

Self-assessment 3 ·

20 mins

1   Here is some performance information for two factories owned by the same organization. They both make Product X. The figures show the numbers of units of Product X produced by each factory. Your task is to produce a numerical comparison of the performance of the two factories, and comment on what you find.

	Quarter 1	Quarter 2	Quarter 3	Quarter 4
Factory A	31,200	31,000	34,300	29,800
Factory B	18,500	19,300	16,200	31,700

_____

_____

_____

_____

_____

_____

_____

2   What measures could you devise to assess staff morale amongst your workteam? Try to think of three. Remember that quantitative measures are more useful than qualitative measures.

_____

_____

_____

_____

_____

_____

_____

3   Fill in the missing words in the following sentences.

■   Benchmarking is a good way of avoiding _____ and it may give rise to _____ _____.

■   The main interest of shareholders is to get a _____ on their _____, so _____ is usually thought of as a commercial organization's prime objective.

■   The balanced scorecard looks at an organization from four different points of view.

a _____

b _____

c _____

d _____

Answers to these questions can be found on page 115.

9 Summary

- Performance measurement looks at how well something performs compared with how it performed in the past, or how it is required to perform in the future, or how something else performs.

- Quantitative information is most useful because it gives you a clear target to beat.

- It is important to make sure that you are comparing like with like.

- An organization's performance is judged on profitability, productivity and activity.

- Financial performance indicators compare performance against budget, the trend over time, other organizations, the economy in general and future potential.

- Non-financial measures look at specific aspects, such as the number of people served or the time taken to do something.

- External comparisons can be made against the general economy and competitors, and by benchmarking against competitors, other processes or other internal departments.

- Stakeholders are internal (employees), connected (owners, customers, financiers, suppliers), and external (community, government, pressure groups, professional bodies). Their objectives may be in conflict.

- The balanced scorecard is a performance measurement framework that takes account of the interests of all stakeholders.

Session D
Monitoring and improving performance

1 Introduction

In this session we are going to see how you could actually set up a performance management system for your own department, and what you might do with it once it was in place.

Here's an outline of a series of steps to follow in establishing and operating your own system.

- **Set performance standards**
  Decide what you need to measure the performance of, then define what is meant by 'performance', and what is 'acceptable performance'.

- **Monitor performance**
  Devise ways of measuring performance that show you whether or not you are performing to the standard expected. Create a system to collect the information you'll need to calculate the measures, and then put it into practice: collect the information and calculate the measures on a regular basis. Finally, report them to the people who need to know.

- **Improve performance**
  Following performance reports, take appropriate action so that you maintain, and hopefully improve, performance in the future.

2 Developing performance standards

A performance 'standard' is a performance measure that says a particular level of performance should be achieved.

If you heard something described simply as 'standard' you would expect it to be no better or worse than another, acceptable example of the same thing. If you heard about 'high standards', you would expect something better than what is usually expected.

Setting performance standards is a three-part process.

- Define what it is you are measuring.
- Find out what is acceptable.
- Establish a level of performance as the standard.

2.1 What are you measuring?

So what 'performance' is it that you will be measuring? To answer this question you first need to consider the purpose of your part of the organization – that is, what it actually performs.

Activity 45   3 mins

What is the purpose of your part of your organization? Avoid the temptation to go into detail: define it as simply as you can.

_____

_____

_____

_____

A short and simple phrase or sentence will do as an answer. Here are some examples I've thought of.

- We assemble the engines that form part of products X, Y and Z.
- We answer general correspondence and deal with telephone calls from customers.
- We create artwork and computer graphics for company publications.
- We process claims on household contents insurance policies.

2.2 What is 'acceptable' performance?

We saw earlier that performance means different things to different people.

Activity 46

Who are your workteam's particular stakeholders?

What aspects of your workteam's performance matter to them?

Here are some possible stakeholders for an individual workteam that I have thought of. Perhaps you came up with the same ones?

- **Customers**
  Even if you do not deal directly with the people who buy your organization's products and services, you still have customers in the sense that someone (an internal customer) uses the output of your department in the next stage of the process.

  Whether they are internal or external, customers are concerned that your output should be delivered when they need it, and be free of faults. That is their standard for you.

■ **Senior managers**
They expect to see your department comply with the organization's rules and policies, such as hours of work ('all staff will work from 9 to 5 and take one hour for lunch between 12 am and 2 pm').

■ **External stakeholders**
They may be involved, for instance if your work requires you to follow certain rules and procedures prescribed by the government. A payroll department is a good example: they have to follow rules and meet deadlines set by the Inland Revenue, to the letter.

■ **Your colleagues and you yourself**
You are all internal stakeholders, of course, and you will be concerned about matters such as levels of pay, how enjoyable and absorbing the work is, opportunities for career progression, and so on.

Individuals have different standards for these things.

2.3 Setting standards

Armed with as much information as you can glean from stakeholders, you can now begin to set standards.

Wherever you can, quantify the information. For instance, if customers expect 'fast' delivery but don't specify what they mean by 'fast', you can find out how quickly your department delivers on average.

You then have a choice of whether to use that average, based on current working conditions, as the initial standard, or whether to be more ambitious.

■ Attainable (or 'expected') standards are based on the premise that work will be carried out efficiently, equipment will be properly operated and materials will be properly used. An allowance can be made for inefficiencies if there is no way of avoiding them, given current working conditions.

■ Ideal standards are based on perfect operating conditions: no inefficiencies, no lost or wasted time, no machine breakdowns or computer crashes, no wasted or spoiled materials.

We'll come back to this choice later. For now, assume that we have decided to be realistic and set standards that we know are attainable.

Activity 47

3 mins

A call centre has the following information about how long 10 examples of a particular type of customer query took to be resolved during a period of one week.

Call	Minutes
1	1
2	5
3	6
4	7
5	9
6	6
7	8
8	5
9	6
10	7

The call centre has set a performance standard that says that 95% of all such queries should be resolved within the standard time set.

What is the standard time? (Add up the times and divide by the number of calls measured.)

_____

How many times did the call centre meet the standard (i.e. the query took the standard time or less to be resolved).

_____

Did the company meet its standard during the week in question?

_____

I calculated that the times add up to 60. As the number of calls is 10, the standard time is 6 minutes. You can see this is attainable because some calls took less time than this.

Unfortunately only six out of the ten calls were completed within the standard time. This is 6/10 × 100% = 60% of calls, so the company is failing to achieve its standard of 95% by a long way.

3 Monitoring performance

In theory you could monitor performance simply by asking your stakeholders now and then to tell you what they think, but this does not give you much control over what is going on.

A much better approach is to record relevant activities of your department as they happen, and then analyse and review the performance measures on a regular basis.

The issue of collecting information and analysing it is covered in depth in other workbooks in this series: *Collecting Information* and *Information in Management.*

Computers or computerized machines can collect a mass of data about how much time and other resources are used on any task. But to analyse such data requires your time and effort.

Indeed, the cost of collecting the information required to produce a performance should be carefully weighed up against the benefits of having that particular measure.

3.1 Measuring performance against standards

Let's say your customers expect fast delivery of your department's output, and you have calculated that **on average** it takes two days for your workteam to produce the output. You are thinking about using this as the standard.

It is only an **average** figure, so sometimes it must take longer than two days, and sometimes it must take less. Really, it would be better if the performance standard was: '**guaranteed** delivery within **no more than** two days', but to achieve this, the work of your department probably needs to be analysed in more detail.

You need to identify all the processes and inputs involved in performing tasks, and the relationships between them; you need to find out what is normal; and then you need to use measures to see where failures and errors occur.

This may not be information that you calculate on a regular basis, but information that you **could** calculate if there has been some variance from expected performance, and you need to interpret the numbers and investigate the cause.

The measures you might calculate to do this for a particular area of performance will often combine and compare measures from the chart shown below.

Common measures of areas of performance	
Area of performance	**Common measures**
Error or failure	Absenteeism/sickness rates Complaints received Defects detected Incidents of equipment failure Time spent waiting or time late Miscalculations made Misinformation given Returned goods received Incidents of being out of stock Claims under warranties
Time taken	Measured per second, minute, hour, day, week, month or year Measured per shift or cycle
Quantity produced etc.	Range of products made Number of parts/components held Units produced Units sold Services performed Kg/litres/metres of product produced Number of documents produced or processed Deliveries made Enquiries received
People's activities	Number of employees Range of employee skills Number of repeat customers Size of competitors Rabge of suppliers

You can use this chart in a number of ways to create a very large number of performance measures, simply by inserting the word 'per'.

- Compare items in different columns, for instance 'Absenteeism per employee' or 'Equipment failures per day'.
- Compare items in the same column, for instance litres (of some resource) used per unit produced'. 'Documents produced per service performed' might show you that a particular task seemed to generate an unusually large amount of paperwork: something worth investigating by looking at that task and the associated documents themselves.

You can also combine elements in more elaborate ways: for instance you might be interested to know the number of units sold by a particular employee per month compared with the total number of units sold by all employees in that month.

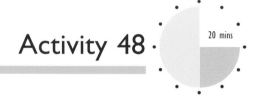

Activity 48

20 mins

S/NVQ D1.1

This activity may provide the basis of appropriate evidence for your S/NVQ portfolio. If you are intending to take this course of action it might be better to write your answers on separate sheets of paper.

The common performance measures chart that we have just seen is not all-inclusive of course, so you need to make it more useful to you in your work.

Adapt some of the common performance measures so that they are relevant to your workteam: for 'range of products', for instance, you could substitute specific products made or services provided by your workteam. You will need to delete some items as not being relevant.

- Using your personalized chart, devise at least four performance measures that might be useful to help you manage your department.

- Explain why they might be useful.

- Explain how you would collect the information relevant to your performance measures.

Obviously I don't know which measures would be useful in your situation, but here are some suggestions, showing ways of using the chart.

- 'Miscalculations per 1,000 invoices' would show how accurately someone in the Accounts Department was working.
- 'Defects per item returned' may show that poor-quality goods are being sold or (if there are no defects in returned goods) that customers' real needs are not being properly identified.

- 'Misinformation per 100 customer enquiries' may show you how knowledgeable and well-trained your customer service staff are.
- 'Customers waiting per minute' shows you how long the queue in your shop is.

3.2 Being realistic

Of course, one way of dealing with a failure to meet a performance standard is to set a **lower** standard!

Obviously that is not desirable in the long term, but there may be occasions when there is no other option because of matters that are outside your control.

For example, if your department requires a certain number of highly-trained people to operate effectively and there is a sudden flu epidemic, the chances are that you will fail to meet your normal standards for a time.

The best thing to do is to be totally open about it. At the earliest opportunity, tell everyone who relies on your department's performance that you won't meet your targets. Then they have the chance to make alternative arrangements or, if none can be made, to alert their own customers to the fact that things have been held up.

There are other situations in which standards might be revised. For example, the standard time for doing a task using a certain piece of equipment might change when a new version of the equipment is acquired. It would be meaningless to compare current performance using the new equipment with the old standard.

On the other hand, if you change standards too frequently, people might think you are constantly 'moving the goal posts'. Your staff will not be motivated to perform well if they can never reach the standard required. This is the problem with so-called 'ideal standards', mentioned earlier.

I would say that you should adjust standards when changes of a permanent nature occur, but not in response to temporary 'blips'.

3.3 Performance reports

Performance reports should be produced and examined as often as they are needed. Your managers might want to see a report once a week or once a month, because they assume you have everything pretty much under control.

You might want to see a report at the end of each day, or perhaps more often, to make sure that you really do have things under control.

There is no prescribed format for a performance report: it will be different for each organization and each part of the organization.

■ You may be able to call up a detailed list of performance measures on a computer screen and just glance through the latest figures to reassure yourself about specific issues.

■ Your manager is not likely to want to see a report that goes into a great amount of detail, especially about things that have performed as expected, as most generally do. But he or she will be interested in 'exceptions' – the one or two things that went wrong – and you may well be required to add comments explaining why those things went wrong, and what you have done about it.

Activity 49 · 5 mins

Here is an extract from the performance information available about the work of a sales order processing department. There are 12 people in the department and they work a seven-hour day, five days a week, mostly dealing with orders submitted on paper, though they also deal with some telephone orders.

	Expected	Actual
Staff-hours available	420	440
Orders processed	1500	1450
Calls received	120	130
Returns processed	15	10

As a general rule 'exceptions' are only reported to senior managers when the difference from the expected or target figure is more than 5%.

Which of these figures might senior managers be most interested in, and why?

_____

_____

_____

_____

If you calculate the percentages, you'll find that calls received ((130−120)/120 × 100% = 8.3% more) and returns processed ((15−10)/15 × 100% = 75% less) were both outside the limit. On the other hand, there was not an unmanageably large number of extra calls, and it is good news that there were fewer than expected returns (although actually there might have been many, but they did not get processed at all). Also, both are outside the control of the workteam being measured, so the manager is unlikely to be greatly interested.

Do you agree that the most unusual thing in this report is that there were about 4% more staff-hours available than there should have been (12 × 7 × 5 = 420). This means that the department worked some overtime or had some extra help. Why should they need to do so, since it was a pretty average week?

The lesson here is to try to think like your manager would think (or whoever you are reporting to). Don't just follow the rules blindly: take an overview and think about whether the figures make sense when considered in relation to each other.

4 Improving performance

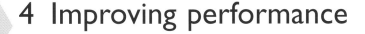

Let's say that you have a complete set of standards which you are monitoring and reporting on. Is this the end of the process?

No, of course we want to improve performance, and some of the processes that we have just gone through will help us to do this.

4.1 Continuous improvement

In modern organizations it is not enough just to perform to the same standard all the time, even if that standard was originally a good one.

- In commercial organizations at least, competition is fierce: if you just stand still, your competitors will come out with a better product and take your share of the market.
- Technology is changing and advancing faster than ever before, creating new opportunities and making old ways of doing things obsolete.
- Customers have learned to expect higher and higher quality.

The emphasis in modern organizations, therefore, is on continuous improvement. This is essentially about reviewing what you do, identifying problems or areas for improvement, planning and implementing the improvements, reviewing the effects of the improvements, identifying further areas for improvement, and so on.

Relating this to the measurement of performance against standards, we can think of it as a cycle with the following six steps.

1   Set standards and formulate performance measures.

2   Monitor against standards and performance measures (by asking for feedback from stakeholders such as customers and employees, and collecting information relating to performance measures).

3   Identify areas of non-conformance to standards and poor performance, and collect further data.

4   Plan improvements (by identifying possible causes of non-conformance and poor performance and discussing solutions).

5   Implement improvements (in inputs, processes or outputs).

6   Set higher standards and updated performance measures and monitor these (in other words, go back to step 2 again).

We've looked at steps 1 to 4 already. In this section we'll concentrate on step 5 and suggest lots of things that you can either do yourself in your department, or recommend to more senior managers, to make a contribution to the continuous improvement of your organization.

We'll think mainly about improving the performance of a small part of an organization that takes inputs from one department and passes its outputs to another part of the organization.

An example would be a department that takes engine parts and components, assembles the engine, and then passes it to a department that connects the engine up to the car body. Another example would be a department that takes applications for credit from a customer services department, checks the credit status of the applicant, and then passes the application on for final approval by a team in head office.

To help us look at different aspects of performance we'll think in terms of a system.

A system is something that takes **inputs** and performs **processes** on those inputs to produce **outputs**. For example, a bread-making system takes flour, yeast and water (inputs), mixes them up, kneads the mixture, makes it rise and bakes it (processes), and produces loaves of bread (outputs).

Any aspect of work can be seen in this way. In fact an organization as a whole can be seen as a system.

4.2 Improving inputs

The inputs of a department are the resources it uses to make outputs. They include materials, machines and office equipment, information, and above all the people you manage.

We'll save the especially complex issue of people for a separate section and confine our comments here to ways you can improve the performance you get out of other inputs.

■ Find better suppliers for inputs, who can deliver better-quality items, or deliver faster, or more consistently on time, or in more convenient quantities, or who offer a better after-sales support service. Price is always an issue, too, of course: it is good to save money, but remember cheaper supplies may be inferior.

■ Don't regard suppliers as 'the enemy': develop closer partnerships with suppliers so that they understand your needs better.

■ If external information is a key input (for example, information about stock markets, or other companies' activities, or the economic climate in another country) you need that information to be the most up-to-date and accurate available, but you don't need to be overwhelmed. You could subscribe to a specialist information service such as Reuters, who will tailor the information they have available to your precise needs.

■ If inputs to your department are outputs from another department, then you are that department's customer, and you are entitled to express your views about the quality of their work. Again, it is better to view the relationship as a partnership, not as a fight. Perhaps there are ways of improving the layout of the forms on which they supply information to you, or perhaps you could share a database with them to make it easier to exchange information. Perhaps they could give you early warning about any delays in delivery.

Activity 50

4 mins

You are the manager in charge of the team who operate the checkouts of a medium-sized branch of a supermarket. (It will help if you think about the supermarket you and your family use personally.)

Identify the resources that are the inputs to the checkout process, and recommend at least one way of improving those inputs. (Concentrate on inputs – we'll think about processes and outputs in the next two activities).

_____

_____

_____

_____

_____

_____

These are the checkout inputs in my local supermarket.

- The people who operate the checkouts, and their time, skill and knowledge.
- Equipment and 'stationery', including computerized tills and paper till rolls, a conveyor belt, a bar code scanner, a number pad for keying in bar codes that cannot be scanned, a set of electronic scales, a credit card scanner, and a tool for removing security tags from items such as clothing.
- Information from a system that links up barcodes to product descriptions and prices.
- The notes and coins in the tills.
- The supermarket goods chosen by customers (food, toiletries etc.) and plastic bags for them to be carried home.

I think the most obvious ways of improving checkout inputs at my supermarket would be to:

- have more checkout desks open, which means employing more people;
- have scanners that work more of the time;
- have a machine that automates the packing of bags, which I hate, and which holds everyone up.

You might have thought of other improvements to inputs: better training for staff, more bar-coded items, a machine that would allow customers to scan in their purchases themselves, or better maintenance and regular cleaning of the conveyor belts – and possibly a host of others, depending what most annoys you about your supermarket!

4.3 Improving processes

There are lots of ways to improve processes. Here are some suggestions.

■ Stop doing unnecessary things just because 'that's the way we've always done it', or 'that's what it says in the procedures manual'.

Although it can be quite a time-consuming exercise, it is worth describing on paper each operation that people in your department perform, and then critically analysing each one. Can you eliminate any activity altogether? Can you combine activities in some way that avoids double-handling? Do you collect information that you never use (I know I do).

■ Look at your competitors' processes if you can (in other words, benchmark) and simply make sure you start doing things their way if it is better than what you do now. Even if you can't get sufficient competitor information, there may be other departments in your own organization that are worth looking at, especially if your organization has other regional offices or offices overseas.

■ Consider contracting out to external suppliers any processes that don't absolutely have to be done in-house (outsourcing). This allows you to concentrate on what you do best.

■ Change the layout of the work area and storage space to ensure that people who frequently need to work together on a process are physically close to each other and to the things they need to do their jobs.

■ Use computer technology to its full potential, especially to automate routine tasks. If a task is repetitive and boring it is almost certainly possible to program a computer to do it, or at least most of it.

■ Integrate processes with other departments. Look at the department handling the stages of the work prior to your department's involvement. It may be more efficient for your department to take over the last part of their processing, or for the other department to take on the first part of yours. The same could apply to the next department's operations.

■ Look for ways to smooth out operations so that staff members aren't idle at some times and impossibly busy at others. For instance, can you do some of the work in advance of when it would normally be done?

Activity 51

4 mins

Remember you are the manager of the checkout team in a medium-sized branch of a supermarket.

Identify the processes that occur when customers pass through the checkout and recommend at least one way of improving the existing processes.

These are the main processes that I would identify.

- **Calculate the amount owed by the customer**
  Mostly this means picking up an item, finding the bar code, passing it over the scanner and then giving it back to the customer. The computer does the actual calculation. However, there will be a variety of sub-processes to deal with things that don't have a bar code, things whose bar codes can't be read, items that are reduced because they are close to their sell-by date, items that have some damage that is only discovered at the checkout and so on.

- **Take payment from the customer**
  There will be separate sub-processes to deal with payment by cash, cheque, or credit/debit card, processing customer loyalty cards, handling money-off coupons and so on.

- **Give cash back to the customer, if required**
  This process requires the additional input of a signature or initials from the customer and the checkout operator if a credit or debit card is involved.

- **Liaison with colleagues and managers**
  There will be processes for alerting the manager when queues are getting too long, helping out other checkout operators if they run out of change, getting replacements from the shelves for damaged items etc.

- **Update accounting systems and warehousing systems**
  This process is done at the checkout, but in most supermarkets it is entirely automated.

I would say this scenario is one that offers excellent opportunities for benchmarking: just go and shop in another supermarket, and note anything that they do particularly well. Other possible ideas include changing the location or layout of the checkouts, or changing the queuing system so that there is only one queue and the next person in the queue goes to the next available checkout.

4.4 Improving outputs

Your outputs are the products you produce or the services you provide for your internal and/or external customers.

Lots of general things can be done to improve outputs.

- Keep checking that you know who your customers are and what they want. Maybe your work is received later in the process by a department that has no direct contact with yours, and perhaps does not even know that you are responsible for it. Find out what happens to your work after it leaves you, and if there are extra things you could do, or things you could do differently.

- Be more flexible: be willing to tailor your product or service to meet special customer demands.

- See if you can remove any unnecessary parts of the product (for instance decorative features) or pieces of information that are rarely used, so that the product is easier and quicker to create.

- If you produce several different outputs do they, or could they have, any parts or features in common, or use very similar information? If so, you may be able to save time by using the same component for both products. A simple example would be using the same document template for all the reports you produce.

- Think about how your product is delivered. If it is information, you can probably deliver it by internal or external e-mail, or perhaps not deliver it physically at all, just make it available on an intranet. If it is a physical product, you may be able to find a faster or more reliable carrier (rail rather than road, for instance). You may find that customers would prefer to come and collect the product. You may even be able to move your department so that it is nearer your customers.

Yet again you are the manager in charge of the checkout team at a medium-sized branch of a supermarket.

Identify the outputs of the checkout process and recommend at least one way of improving the outputs.

_____

_____

_____

_____

_____

_____

These are my suggestions for outputs.

- The service itself, in other words a customer who has been served in a certain length of time.
- A till receipt and perhaps some money-off coupons.
- Cash back.
- Answers to customer queries such as 'are you open over the Bank Holiday?'
- Occasional help with packing and carrying shopping bags.
- Assistance to colleagues and managers.
- Information for other systems, such as the accounting system, the stock control system and the marketing system.

Most customers will want faster service above all, and there are lots of ways of achieving this, such as 'six items or less' queues and bag packers (assuming they do this more quickly, and as well as, the customer would).

I would like my supermarket to have someone in the checkout area to go and fetch items that I have forgotten to pick up, so I don't lose my place in the queue!

As usual, you probably have your own ideas, depending on your particular gripe with your supermarket.

4.5 Improving staff performance

In 'staff' we include you, of course, because a large part of getting better performance out of people is improving your own management skills. Good management on your part should give you highly motivated and skilled employees. They will work hard for your organization because they realize that if they contribute to your aims, they can achieve their own goals.

You may like to refer to two other Super Series titles: Planning, Training and Development and Delivering Training.

■ Train your staff. Your organization and its environment are continually changing, so employees constantly need to develop new skills. Training may be needed in a variety of areas: in knowledge about the organization (its mission, objectives, systems, other departments); in personal skills such as time management, decision-making, and communication; in specialized knowledge about specific processes in your department or specific tools or software packages that you use; and in general knowledge about matters such as health and safety.

■ Empower your staff. Empowerment means delegating to the lowest possible level, because those most closely involved with operations (the ones who actually do the tasks) are in the best position to make decisions about them. Empowerment leads to faster decisions, helps personal development, and offers staff more job satisfaction.

■ Acknowledge each person's contribution publicly: you'd be surprised how much difference a simple 'thank you' can make. If you are in a position to do so, see that extra effort is rewarded in some way.

■ Encourage teamwork and co-operation. More experienced staff will help with training their less experienced colleagues if both depend on each other to get a job done.

■ Be more open in your communications. Some managers think knowledge is power, but if you keep secrets from people you have no right to be surprised if they don't achieve what you really wanted them to achieve.

■ Think about how you make decisions and whether you can improve. Decisions should be given the attention they deserve, but it is easy to get bogged down in detail.

For more guidance on managing conflict see Managing Lawfully – People and Employment.

■ You can't always make people 'happy', and 'happy' workers aren't necessarily more productive workers. But you can try to make sure that your staff members are treated courteously, without favouritism, prejudice, or public criticism. If you slip, as you probably will, be sure to apologise. If you become aware of a conflict between individual members of staff, bring them together and do everything you can to resolve the conflict. There is nothing worse than an 'atmosphere'.

Activity 53 ·

3 mins

How can you find out whether people need training to improve performance? (You don't have to answer this in relation to the supermarket checkout, but do so if you wish.)

_____

_____

_____

_____

_____

Sometimes it will be obvious. If a new law is passed that affects what an organization does, or new equipment or software is brought in, staff will need to know about it.

Sometimes you may only have hints: absenteeism, high staff turnover, disciplinary issues and frequent mistakes are matters that need to be investigated to see what the root causes are. Training may solve the problem.

Some organizations do formal 'training needs analysis', where training needs are defined as the gap between the requirements of the job and the actual current performance of the people who do it.

Activity 54 ·

30 mins

S/NVQs A1.3, B1.2

This activity may provide the basis of appropriate evidence for your S/NVQ portfolio. If you are intending to take this course of action it might be better to write your answers on separate sheets of paper.

Most of the organization management initiatives that have become popular in the last decade or so have, at heart, the idea of the organization as a system made up of lots of smaller interrelated systems and processes.

Describe your part of your organization in this way, in other words identify your workteam's inputs, processes and outputs.

Can you identify any way in which these inputs, processes and outputs could be changed so that work activities can be improved? Try to identify ways in which resources can be better controlled by making these changes.

4.6 Quality management initiatives

The need to improve performance is fundamental to most modern organizations, and it won't only be your workteam that is expected to improve. The initiative will probably come from very senior managers and will run right through the organization.

Let's look quickly at three organization-wide approaches that you may be expected to contribute to.

■ **Total Quality Management (TQM)**
TQM is a philosophy that the only acceptable quality is perfect quality. This applies to every single resource, process and relationship in the entire organization.

EXTENSION 5
If you want to remove some of the theory, and get some good anecdotes, try *101 Ways to Improve Business Performance* by D. Waters. It's also available as an e-book.

The cost of preventing mistakes is less than the cost of correcting them once they occur. The aim should therefore be to 'get it right first time'.

And even if you do get it right, there is always scope for improvement. The idea of continuous improvement (getting it more right, next time) is a key part of TQM.

■ **ISO 9000**
The ISO 9000 family of standards are set by the International Organization for Standardization, and describe how an organization can set up 'quality management systems' to ensure that quality and customer focus is at the heart of everything the organization does.

If there is a TQM or ISO 9000 initiative in your organization you may find it helpful to look at another workbook in this series, *Achieving Quality*, which covers both in detail.

Organizations that meet ISO 9000's very detailed requirements can arrange to be audited by ISO 9000 Registrars, and get a third-party certificate if they pass.

ISO 9000 is especially important because some types of customer refuse to do business with an organization unless there is some independent assurance of quality. For instance, many government departments and local authorities will only offer contracts to companies that are ISO 9000 certified.

■ **The Business Excellence Model**

The Business Excellence Model is promoted in the UK by the British Quality Foundation. The model is now more properly known as The EFQM Excellence Model, EFQM being the European Foundation for Quality Management. Organizations can enter an annual competition and win awards for business excellence.

The EFQM Excellence Model, a non-prescriptive framework based on nine criteria, can be used to assess an organization's progress towards excellence. The Model recognizes there are many approaches to achieving sustainable excellence in all aspects of performance. It is based on the premise that:

> **excellent results with respect to Performance, Customers, People and Society are achieved through Leadership driving Policy and Strategy, People, Partnerships and Resources and Processes.**

The model is summarized in the diagram below.

Diagram © EFQM, The EFQM Excellence Model is a registered trademark. Explanatory text © EFQM.

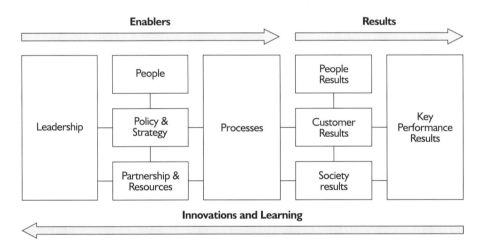

The arrows emphasize the dynamic nature of the model. They show that innovation and learning help to improve enablers which in turn lead to improved results.

For convenience, we use the terms 'Enablers' and 'Results' to designate two catregories of criteria. Enabler criteria are concerned with how the organization undertakes key activities; Results criteria are concerned with what results are being achieved.

Applying the model

We can only give a very simplified idea of the model here. More information, including useful free documents to download, is available from the EFQM website on www.efqm.org. The sort of questions you might ask, just to see how well your organization is performaing in relation to the criteria shown in the diagram, include the following.

I How do the behaviour and actions of the executive team and all other leaders inspire, support and promote a culture of Total Quality Management?

2 How does the organization formulate strategies and turn them into plans and actions?

3 How does the organization release the full potential of its people?

4 How does the organization manage resources (especially financial resources) effectively and efficiently?

5 How does the organization deliver value for customers through the management of its processes?

6 What results is the organization achieving in relation to the satisfaction of its external customers?

7 What results is the organization achieving in relation to the satisfaction of its own people?

8 What results is the organization achieving in satisfying the needs and expectations of the community in which it is located?

9 What results is the organization achieving in relation to its planned organization objectives and in satisfying the needs and expectations of everyone with a financial interest in the organization?

Activity 55

3 mins

To which of the questions in the Business Excellence Model might you give the answer 'via a budgeting system'.

I would say questions 2, 4 and 9 in particular might be answered in this way.

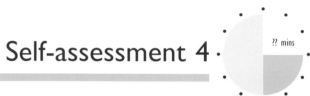

Self-assessment 4

1 Who are your internal customers?

   _____

   _____

   _____

2 What is an ideal standard, and what is the drawback of an ideal standard?

   _____

   _____

   _____

3 Fill in the missing words in the following sentences.

   a Monitoring performance is a way of keeping _____ over the activities you are responsible for.

   b When there is a variance from expected performance you should use measures to see where _____ occurred.

4 What should you do if you cannot meet a performance standard due to circumstances beyond your control?

   _____

   _____

   _____

5 Why should improvement be continuous?

   _____

   _____

   _____

   _____

6 Suggest three ways of improving processes.

   _____

   _____

   _____

Answers to these questions can be found on page 116.

5 Summary

- To set a performance standard you first need to define performance in overall terms, then find out what is regarded as acceptable performance, and finally define a particular level of performance as the standard.

- The standard set may be an attainable standard – the best you can do at the moment – or you can set more ambitious targets.

- To interpret variances from expected performance standards you first need to identify all the processes and inputs involved in performing tasks, and the relationships between them. You then need to find out what is normal and use measures to see where failures and errors occur.

- Performance reports should concentrate on the exceptions to standard performance.

- Modern organizations need to improve continuously because of fierce competition, ever-changing technology and ever-increasing customer expectations.

- You can see an organization as a system of inputs, processes and outputs. This approach emphasizes that whatever you do has an impact on other parts of the organization.

- You may find yourself taking part in an organization-wide initiative to improve performance such as Total Quality Management, ISO 9000 certification or the EFQM Excellence Model.

Performance checks

1 Quick quiz

Write down your answers in the space below to the following questions on *Budgeting for Better Performance*.

Question 1   Describe what is meant by a budget.

_____

_____

Question 2   State **three** things shown by a cash budget.

_____

_____

_____

Question 3   What is likely to be the most common budget in an established business organization?

_____

Question 4   A budget is of value because it can be used to control activities. What is compared with planned outcome to achieve this?

_____

Question 5   Name an organization that uses bed occupancy as a limiting budget factor.

_____

Question 6   What is meant by a variance?

_____

_____

Question 7   Briefly explain what is meant by 'non-controllable' costs.

_____

_____

_____

Question 8   Sales of 200 units at £150 each a week are expected. In the first week, a strong demand means that 250 units are actually sold at £160 each. Calculate the sales variance and indicate whether it is favourable or adverse.

_____

_____

_____

Question 9   Briefly explain the difference between fixed and variable costs.

_____

_____

Question 10   State the difference between budgets and standard costs.

_____

_____

Question 11   What should performance be compared with?

_____

_____

Question 12   What is qualitative information?

_____

_____

Question 13   If a product has to be perfectly spherical, how might you measure the extent to which the required standard is met over a period of time?

_____

_____

Question 14   Give four examples of connected stakeholders.

_____

_____

Question 15   Who decides what is acceptable performance?

_____

_____

Question 16   Why should performance standards be quantified wherever possible?

_____

_____

Question 17   When might a standard be revised?

_____

_____

Answers to these questions can be found on page 118.

60 mins

2 Workbook assessment

Read the following case incident and then deal with the questions that follow, writing your answers on a separate sheet of paper.

Dickens Ltd manufactures a single product. Here is the company's budgeted performance for the month of March.

Production budget:

Sales	20,000 units at £10·00

Materials	£60,000
Labour	£40,000
Maintenance cost	£10,000
Management salaries	£25,000
Rent and rates	£25,000
Other costs	£36,000

Production actual:

Sales	37,500 units at £8·00

Materials	£85,000
Labour	£45,000
Maintenance costs	£14,000
Management salaries	£27,000
Rent and rates	£26,000
Other costs	£50,000

1   Produce a budgetary control report comparing:

a budgeted to actual sales;
b budgeted to actual costs;
c budgeted to actual profit.

Remember that every variance should be followed by (F) Favourable or (A) Adverse.

2 Show how the sales revenue variance can be broken down into:

a sales price variance;
b sales volume variance.

3 Suppose in the above budgeted information the following cost information was available:

a materials, labour and maintenance costs are regarded as variable;
b rent and rates and management salaries are regarded as fixed;
c 'other costs' consist of fixed costs (£16,000) and variable costs (£1·00 per unit produced and sold).

Produce a budgetary control report which takes into account this information about fixed and variable costs.

4 Briefly say what you think the advantages of a flexible budget system would be in this case.

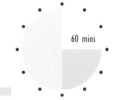

3 Work-based assignment

S/NVQs
B1.1, B1.2
D1.1, D1.2

The time guide for this assignment gives you an approximate idea of how long it is likely to take you to write up your findings. You will need to spend some additional time gathering information, perhaps talking to colleagues and thinking about the assignment. The result of your efforts should be presented on separate sheets of paper.

Your written response to this assignment may provide the basis of appropriate evidence for your S/NVQ portfolio.

There may be some form of budgetary control in your workplace.

Describe the system used for budgets, and any standard costing used in your workplace. Identify any shortcomings in the present system and think of ways these might be improved without damaging the successful aspects of the system.

Explain to your immediate manager and your workteam that you are researching budgetary control in your workplace, discuss your ideas with them and make a note of their suggestions and objections to change.

Draw up a report covering the following questions.

1   Who has direct responsibility for the budget in your work area, and to whom is that person directly responsible?

2   Describe how information about actual performance (e.g. actual costs) is fed back to you and your workteam.

3   Do you think the feedback of information to you could be improved so that you could be more involved in budgetary control? If so, briefly suggest how this could be done.

4   Describe what happens if actual performance does not correspond to budget. Are you or your workteam held to be responsible in any way?

5   How do you feel resources can be better managed?

6   How can changes to the budgetary control system be introduced with the minimum of objections?

If your workplace has no clear budgetary control system, then prepare recommendations for your manager on what form one should take.

Write up your findings and draw up an action plan for you and your workteam. Discuss this with your manager.

Reflect and review

1 Reflect and review

Now that you have completed your work on *Budgeting for Better Performance*, let us review our workbook objectives.

The first objective is:

■ that you should be better able to describe what a budget is.

We've seen that a budget is a financial plan prepared in advance of a certain period. Every department in a business organization is involved in forecasting its budget depending on the level of business activity planned. This can involve a lot of work, but can be a worthwhile investment if the budget is regarded, not as a financial straight-jacket, but as a valuable management tool for planning and controlling.

■ As a first line manager, can you think of improvements in planning and control in your work area that you could suggest to your manager? Make notes of any matters which come to mind below.

_____

_____

_____

_____

_____

■ What are the advantages of budgeting to you and your workteam? Make a note of these if you feel you need to emphasize them.

_____

_____

_____

The second workbook objective was:

■ that you should be better able to understand how budgets are used.

A budget is an expensive exercise unless it is constantly used during the period it relates to. We've seen that it can be used to compare actual performance with planned performance, and flexed to take into account changes in circumstances, or to forecast what will happen in certain circumstances and to make plans accordingly. It also helps management to set targets which ensure the profitability of the organization.

■ Can you think of ways to improve the way budgets are used in your workplace? Make a note of any suggestions you have for change.

_____

_____

_____

■ Are any budgets you use at work flexed to an appropriate extent? Write down your thoughts for future discussions with your manager.

_____

_____

_____

The third workbook objective was:

■ that you should be better able to use some budgetary control techniques.

Looking at fairly simple examples, we've used some budgetary control techniques which would be used in your workplace. These include flexible budgeting and standard costing. If you are involved in setting the budget in your work area or are on a budget committee, the work you have done in this workbook should have increased the confidence with which you handle the techniques.

■ Make a note of techniques you could use in assisting your planning and control.

_____

_____

_____

_____

_____

The next workbook objectives were:

■ that you should be better able to identify ways of measuring performance levels; and

■ that you should be better able to describe a range of methods for measuring performance.

Performance measures should always be considered in relation to something: usually past performance, desired or expected future performance or the performance of something or somebody else.

You can judge the quality of performance using terms like 'delicious', but this may mean different things to different people. It is far better to use quantitative measures, because these give you a clear target to aim for and hopefully beat. Quantitative measures can be sub-divided into financial measures (budgets and variances) and non-financial measures (times, weights, units of product or service, and so on).

Performance might also be measured against the economy in general or against the performance of competitors. Benchmarking is a useful technique: this compares performance with 'best in class' competitors or other departments.

■ By what means is the performance of your workteam measured at present? Do you have budgetary targets, or time deadlines to meet, or a target number of things to process per day/week/month? If you just cope as best you can with unpredictable daily demand, suggest some ways in which you could take control by making more effort to measure various aspects of performance.

■ Do you know who is regarded as 'best in class' at what they do? If not, find out, and make a note of ways you could discover more about how they operate (e.g. buy their products and experience their performance levels for yourself).

_____
_____
_____
_____
_____

The sixth workbook objective was:

■ that you should be better able to identify the differing objectives of stakeholders in the organization

Stakeholders can be divided into three types: internal stakeholders (employees), connected stakeholders (customers, suppliers, financiers), and external stakeholders (the government, the community). Each of these has their own objectives and they will judge the performance of you and your workteam accordingly.

■ Describe your own stake in your organization.

_____
_____
_____
_____
_____
_____

■ Who are your internal customers and suppliers, and what are their objectives?

_____
_____
_____
_____
_____
_____

The seventh workbook objective was:

■   that you should be better able to select the ideal performance measure.

There is no single performance measure that suits everybody: it depends on who you are describing performance to and what their stake in the organization is. So the ideal way of measuring performance is the balanced scorecard approach, which considers performance from a variety of perspectives and tries to satisfy everyone.

■   Note down conflicts in the objectives of the different stakeholders in your part of the organization.

_____

_____

_____

_____

_____

■   Now look at the list you have made above and decide who should win, from the point of view of your organization as a whole. (For instance, if your team wants less work and more pay, will that help your organization complete a job on time and within cost, and get more work in the future?) When you've done this, you should be able to prioritize the various performance measures that are applied to your department. Write a list, in order of importance, below.

_____

_____

_____

_____

_____

The eighth workbook objective was:

■ that you should be better able to monitor performance against agreed targets.

To monitor performance you first need to decide what 'performance' actually means (by asking your stakeholders) and then quantify the key measures that demonstrate whether you are performing well or badly. An initial performance 'standard' can be set by finding out what is the average current performance. You will then aim to achieve or beat that standard all the time, not just some of the time. Monitoring will identify 'exceptions' – occasions when you failed to meet the standard – and you should investigate the reasons why this happened.

■ Non-financial information is very useful for investigating failures, but you have to have the information in the first place. What records do you and your workteam currently keep that could be used in performance measurement? Don't forget to include things that are recorded automatically, like the dates of computer files.

_____

_____

_____

_____

_____

■ Make a list of items of additional information about the activities of your workteam that you *could* record, and then go through the list deciding whether it is actually worth recording that information. In other words, decide whether the benefits of having the information outweigh the cost (probably time) of recording it and analysing it.

_____

_____

_____

_____

_____

The final workbook objective was:

■ that you should be better able to make recommendations for improvement in performance, or adjustments to more realistic targets.

Targets can't always be met, often because of circumstances beyond your control. If this is the case, the most important thing is to tell the people you are going to let down as early as possible, and agree a new target that you will be able to meet.

As a general rule, however, businesses should aim to improve continuously, and many adopt organization-wide initiatives such as Total Quality Management or ISO 9000 certification to achieve this.

When looking for areas of improvement, it is helpful to think in terms of inputs, processes and outputs. Think especially about whether things you currently do need to be done at all, whether you can integrate processes (combine them into one) or automate them somehow, and whether you can address people issues such as training and relationships with other departments.

■ What improvements have you made since you took charge of your workteam? Make a note below, and concentrate on things that are quantified.

_____

_____

_____

_____

_____

■ What improvements do the stakeholders in your part of the organization want to see in the future – over the next six months say? If you don't know, ask them (your staff, your own manager, your colleagues in other departments) and make a note of their responses below.

_____

_____

_____

_____

_____

2 Action plan

Use this plan to further develop for yourself a course of action you want to take. Make a note in the left-hand column of the issues or problems you want to tackle, and then decide what you intend to do, and make a note in column 2.

The resources you need might include time, materials, information or money. You may need to negotiate for some of them, but they could be something easily acquired, like half an hour of somebody's time, or a chapter of a book. Put whatever you need in column 3. No plan means anything without a timescale, so put a realistic target completion date in column 4.

Finally, describe the outcome you want to achieve as a result of this plan, whether it is for your own benefit or advancement, or a more efficient way of doing things.

Desired outcomes				
1 Issues	2 Action	3 Resources	4 Target completion
Actual outcomes				

3 Extensions

Extension 1	Book	*The Business Plan Workbook*
	Authors	Colin Barrow, Paul Barrow and Robert Brown
	Edition	Fourth edition, revised 2001
	Publisher	Kogan Page

Extension 2	Book	*Budgeting for Non-Financial Managers*
	Author	Ian Maitland
	Edition	1999
	Publisher	Financial Times Prentice Hall 1999

Extension 3	Book	*Managing Budgets: Essential Managers Series*
	Edition	2000
	Publisher	Dorling Kindersley

Extension 4	Book	*Balanced Scorecard Step-by-Step: Maximizing Performance and Maintaining Results*
	Authors	Paul R Niven and Robert S Kaplan
	Edition	2002
	Publisher	John Wiley & Sons

This book explains how an organization can measure and manage performance with the balanced scorecard methodology. It provides extensive background on performance management and the balanced scorecard, and focuses on guiding a team through the step-by-step development and ongoing implementation of a balanced scorecard system. It's also available as an e-book.

Extension 5	Book	*101 Ways to Improve Business Performance*
	Author	Donald Waters
	Edition	1999
	Publisher	Kogan Page

This book describes ideas for improving business performance, taking the view that the purpose of ev ery organization is to make a product that satisfies customer needs. The text examines management support, product design, quality management, planning, equipment and logistics.

These Extensions can be taken up via your ILM Centre. They will arrange for you to have access to them. However, it may be more convenient to check out the materials with your personnel or training people at work – they could well give you access. There are good reasons for approaching your own people as, by doing so, they will become aware of your continuing interest in the subject and you will be able to involve them in your development.

4 Answers to self-assessment questions

Self-assessment 1 on page 13

1 The four features of a budget are that it:
- is quantitative;
- is prepared in advance;
- relates to a particular period;
- is a plan of action.

2 Budgets are essential for deciding at the outset whether an objective can be achieved and what actions this requires. They also give managers their targets and cost limits for the next period.

3 a Budgets are largely a waste of time unless they are actively USED in order to see whether the organization is MEETING its targets and keeping within its limits.

This helps to ensure that expenditure takes place according to plan.

b We use the term BUDGETARY CONTROL to cover the use of budgets to help an organization control its progress towards what it has set out to achieve.

Setting targets and encouraging people to adhere to them assists the organization through a disciplined approach.

c A budget will not be useful to an organization if it is managed so RIGIDLY that it does not permit some degree of flexibility.

Unless allowances are made for changes in circumstances, organizations can incur expenses and losses in trying to achieve the impossible.

1 The five basic steps of budgetary control systems are to:

- establish agreed budgets;
- report actual results to departmental managers;
- identify where actual performance differs from planned performance using variances;
- agree which department or who is responsible for variances;
- analyse why variances have happened.

2 A favourable variance indicates that actual sales are greater than budgeted sales, or actual costs are less than budgeted costs.

An adverse variance indicates that actual sales are less than budgeted sales, or actual costs are greater than budgeted costs.

3 a The goods purchased and sold by a greengrocer are controllable costs.

b The rent of a chair in a hairdressing salon is non-controllable.

4 The sales variance is calculated as follows.

Budgeted sales revenue 100 × £8·50 = £850
Actual sales revenue   90 × £7·00 = £630

Total sales variance   £220 adverse

(You could analyse the total sales variance as follows.

Volume	10 × £8.50	£85.00	adverse
Price	90 × £1.50	£135.00	adverse
Total		£220.00	adverse)

5 The labour cost variance is:

Budgeted cost 16 × £20·00 = £320
Actual cost   24 × £13·00 = £312

Variance   £8 favourable

(You could analyse the total labour variance as follows.

Volume	8 × £20.00	£160.00	adverse
Price	24 × £7.00	£168.00	favourable
Total		£8.00	favourable)

6 Flexible budgeting provides the opportunity to be able to take account of changes in circumstances and more closely monitor the position than is possible using fixed budgets.

7 The break-even number of tickets to be sold is calculated as:

Sales price	£5.00
Variable costs	£3.00
Contribution per ticket	£2.00

Break-even point = £200.00 ÷ £2.00 = 100 tickets

Self-assessment 3 on page 68

1   Here is an analysis that shows the total production and how much each factory contributes to the total, as a percentage.

	Quarter 1	Quarter 2	Quarter 3	Quarter 4
Factory A	31,200 63%	31,000 62%	34,300 68%	29,800 48%
Factory B	18,500 37%	19,300 38%	16,200 32%	31,700 52%
	49,700	50,300	50,500	61,500

From this you can see that the overall production is reasonably consistent for the first three quarters (about 50,000 units), with Factory A doing most of the work.

In the fourth quarter, production shoots up by about 10,000 units and the two factories do an almost equal amount of work, although in fact it is only Factory B which increases production by a significant amount.

The most likely reason for this is that we are not comparing like with like for the first three quarters. Factory B was probably smaller or less well-equipped, or had some other problems that affected its ability to produce more than 20,000 units. By the time we get to the fourth quarter, Factory B seems to have been brought up to the standard of Factory A.

2   If people keep leaving your organization to go to another job that may be an indication that morale is not very good.

Staff turnover is calculated by dividing the number of leavers by the total number of staff. For instance, if you have a team of 12 people and three leave during the year and are replaced, you have a staff turnover of 3/12 x 100% = 25%.

If people don't like coming to work that may be because of low morale. Absenteeism is measured by comparing the number of days or hours lost in the year compared with the total number of hours that people should have worked.

Your own management activity can also be used as a measure. You could keep a record of the number of times you have to step in to resolve conflicts between members of your team.

Your team members will have their own views and you could ask them to rate morale on a scale of 1 to 10, say.

You may have had other valid ideas.

3   Benchmarking is a good way of avoiding COMPLACENCY and it may give rise to NEW IDEAS.

The main interest of shareholders is to get a RETURN on their INVESTMENT, so PROFITABILITY is usually thought of as a commercial organization's prime objective.

The balanced scorecard looks at an organization from four different points of view.

a CUSTOMER
b INTERNAL
c INNOVATION AND LEARNING
d FINANCIAL

Self-assessment 4 on page 94

1 Your internal customers are the people, or groups of people, in your organization who need the work that you do to enable them to do their job.

2 An ideal standard is based on perfect operating conditions: no inefficiencies, no lost or wasted time, no machine breakdowns or computer crashes, no wasted or spoiled materials.

The disadvantage of an ideal standard is that it's almost impossible to achieve because not everything can be controlled. Staff will not be motivated to perform well if they can never reach the standard required.

3 a Monitoring performance is a way of keeping CONTROL over the activities you are responsible for.
 b When there is a variance from expected performance you should use measures to see where ERRORS, FAILURES AND DEFECTS occurred.

4 The most important thing is to be totally open about it. You should tell everyone who relies on your department's performance at the earliest opportunity that you won't meet your targets. This gives them the opportunity to make alternative arrangements.

5 Improvement should be continuous because:

- if you just stand still your competitors will come out with a better product and take your share of the market;
- technology is changing and advancing faster than ever before, creating new opportunities and making old ways of doing things obsolete;
- customers have come to expect higher and higher quality.

6 Here are three possible ways to improve processes (other answers may be equally valid).

- Integrate with other processes.
- Automate routine tasks.
- Consider whether they can be eliminated completely.

5 Answers to activities

**Activity 15
on page 26**

Budgeted material cost = 1,000 kilos × £3·00 = £3,000.
Actual material cost = 1,200 kilos × £2·50 = £3,000.
Variance = nil

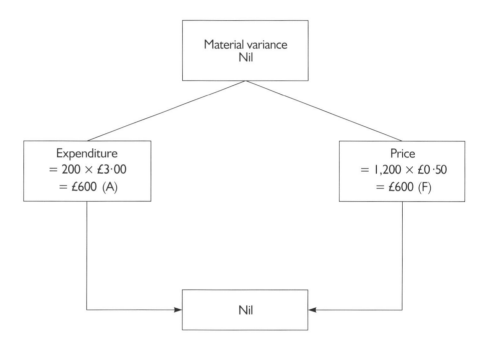

In this case, the lower price exactly counters the extra cost from using 200 kilos more than were budgeted for.

6 Answers to the quick quiz

Answer 1   A budget is a quantitative plan of action prepared in advance of a defined period of time.

Answer 2   A cash budget shows:

- the cash received and paid out during the budget period;
- the timing of receipts and payments;
- the bank balance or overdraft at the end of each month.

Answer 3   The sales budget.

Answer 4   Actual outcome.

Answer 5   A hotel or hospital.

Answer 6   The difference between actual and planned performance.

Answer 7   Costs charged to a budget centre, but which cannot be influenced by the activities of people responsible for that budget centre.

Answer 8   Budgeted sales revenue 200 × £150 = £30,000
Actual sales revenue   250 × £160 = £40,000

Sales variance   £10,000 favourable

Answer 9   Fixed costs do not vary with sales and production. Variable costs do vary.

Answer 10   Budgets are concerned with totals whereas standard costs are concerned with individual units.

Answer 11   Performance should be compared with past performance, desired future performance or the performance of something else.

Answer 12   Qualitative information is information that is not expressed in numerical terms or cannot be expressed in numerical terms in a way that has an agreed meaning.

Answer 13   Measure the number of defective products: for instance three out of every 100 produced are not of the required quality.

Answer 14   Shareholders, suppliers, customers, financiers.

Answer 15   Stakeholders decide, especially customers.

Answer 16   If you have a numerical measure you have a very clear target to aim for and, if possible, beat.

Answer 17   When changes of a permanent nature occur, but not in response to temporary 'blips'. For example, the standard time for doing a task using a certain piece of equipment might change when a new version of the equipment is acquired.

7 Certificate

Completion of this certificate by an authorized person shows that you have worked through all the parts of this workbook and satisfactorily completed the assessments. The certificate provides a record of what you have done that may be used for exemptions or as evidence of prior learning against other nationally certificated qualifications.

Pergamon Flexible Learning and ILM are always keen to refine and improve their products. One of the key sources of information to help this process are people who have just used the product. If you have any information or views, good or bad, please pass these on.

INSTITUTE OF LEADERSHIP & MANAGEMENT

SUPERSERIES

Budgeting for Better Performance

....

has satisfactorily completed this workbook

Name of signatory   ....

Position   ....

Signature   ....

Date   ....

Official stamp

Fourth Edition

INSTITUTE OF LEADERSHIP & MANAGEMENT

SUPER SERIES

FOURTH EDITION

To order – phone us direct for prices and availability details
(please quote ISBNs when ordering) on 01865 888190